Strategies for Change

LYLE E. SCHALLER

Abingdon Press
NASHVILLE

STRATEGIES FOR CHANGE

Copyright © 1993 by Abingdon Press

This book is printed on recycled, acid-free paper.

Library of Congress Cataloging-in-Publication Data

SCHALLER, LYLE E.
    Strategies for change / Lyle E. Schaller.
        p.   cm.
    Includes bibliographical references.
    ISBN 0-687-39673-5 (pbk   :   alk. paper)
        1. Church management.   2. Change—Religious aspects—Christianity.
3. Christian leadership.   I. Title.
    BV652.S357   1993
    254—dc20   92-33159
                                                                                    CIP

92 93 94 95 96 97 98 99 00 01 02 — 10 9 8 7 6 5 4 3 2 1

MANUFACTURED IN THE UNITED STATES OF AMERICA

To Clara and Nicholas

Contents

Contents

Introduction

The story has been told of the faithful, devout, and hard-working Roman Catholic nun who suddenly died as she was completing her fortieth year of teaching in the same parochial school in an inner-city parish. She was ushered into heaven and taken to a large and beautiful classroom that had one wall filled with bookshelves and sunlight streaming in from windows on two sides. It was explained to her the room also was equipped with all of the most advanced technological pedagogical instructional equipment including remote controlled projectors in the ceiling for showing videotapes on a screen, a computer at every desk, and a variety of remote control devices. "Sister, this is where you will spend eternity."

"Oh, no!" she exclaimed. "I wouldn't know what to do here. I spent all my life in a small classroom with plaster walls, a hardwood floor, blackboards, a tiny bookcase for our library, and two pictures on the walls, one of the Pope and the other of George Washington. Every year I was given a new box of chalk and two reams of colored mimeograph paper. Once, about twenty years ago, we got new desks for all the children. That's what I'm used to. I wouldn't know how to teach in a room like this."

"Sorry, Sister," came the reply. "All of those classrooms are down below."

The moral of that story is everyone has two choices—adapt or go to hell. This book has been written for those who prefer the first of those two alternatives.

From a different perspective, another question can be asked. What is the number-one issue facing Christian organizations on the North American continent today? What is the one issue that faces every congregation, denomination, movement, theological seminary, parachurch organization, and interchurch agency? Dwindling numbers? Money? Social justice? Competent leadership? The growing dysfunctional nature of ecclesiastical structures? Television? The new immigration from the Pacific Rim and Latin America? Governmental regulations? Human sexuality? The fact our society has become an increasingly barren and hostile environment for rearing children? The shift from verbal to visual communication?

After more than three decades spent working with thousands of congregational, denominational, seminary, and parachurch leaders from more than five dozen traditions, this observer places a one-sentence issue at the top of that list. The need to initiate and implement planned change from within an organization. That is the number-one issue today for most congregations, denominations, theological seminaries, parachurch organizations, and reform movements.

One subject will illustrate that statement. During the past three decades tens of millions of words have been published on church growth. Countless workshops and seminars have been held to promote church growth. Several denominations have made church growth a high priority.

The Church Growth Movement has produced a huge variety of valuable insights and resources for those interested in promoting numerical growth. Opponents of that movement have marshalled their arguments to explain why this emphasis on numerical growth falls somewhere between heretical and demonic.

The neglected facet of this debate is that numerical growth is not the issue, but rather a product of a larger concern.

The big issue is change. The central issue in any effective strategy for numerical growth—whether by a congregation, a denomination, a theological seminary, or a parachurch organization—

is change. Reversing a period of numerical decline requires changes. Numerical growth also produces change.

From this observer's perspective that means the key to the effective implementation of a church growth strategy is skill as an agent of planned change initiated from within that organization. That often means a change in the priorities in the allocation of scarce resources among competing demands. That may require changes in schedules, staffing, real estate, and other means-to-an-end issues. It may mean a change in the criteria for recruiting and training a new generation of leaders.

Skill at initiating change from within an organization also will be the critical variable in determining which organizations will be most effective in propagating the gospel to new generations in the twenty-first century.

This is the fourth in an Abingdon Press series of five books by this author on planned change. The first, *The Change Agent* (1972), was directed at the individual who seeks to initiate change in any organization. To my surprise and delight, it also was used as a textbook in at least a couple of medical schools that defined the role of physicians as intentional agents of planned change.

The second, *Getting Things Done* (1986), focused on the leadership role and style of individuals. The third, *Create Your Own Future* (1991), was directed at members of long-range planning committees. It covers everything from the reasons for the existence of these special study committees to criteria for selecting the members to the functioning of the committee to preparing and implementing recommendations.[1]

The distinctive focus of this volume is on the institutional context and the climate for change and the sources of the authority required to initiate change. It concludes with suggestions on strategies and tactics.

The fifth and final volume in the series, *The Interventionist,* will be directed at denominational staff members, parish consultants, seminary professors, and others who accept the responsibility for direct on-the-scene intervention in congregational life.

Inasmuch as each volume was and is intended to stand alone, there is some overlap in the material presented. This will be most apparent to those who have read *The Change Agent* and now read the sixth and eighth chapters of this book. Far less overlap will be found by those who have read *Getting Things Done* or *Create Your Own Future!* and this volume. The least overlap will be this book with the forthcoming *The Interventionist.*

The most frequently heard evaluation from pastors or denominational staff members who have just completed a five-day workshop on leadership and planned change is, "I wish I had been taught this in seminary."

That is a predictable comment, but it reflects an unfair and unrealistic expectation.

First, the responsibility of theological seminaries is not to try to teach this and similar subjects. From this observer's perspective the number-one responsibility in theological seminaries should be to cultivate in seminary students a joy in learning, a desire to learn more, and a skill in how to learn. If this can be supplemented by enhancing reading and writing skills, that is half the battle.

The other half of the responsibility of theological seminaries should be to do what they can do best. Ideally theological seminaries will follow the advice of Bishop Herbert Chilstrom who advised the Evangelical Lutheran Church in America Task Force on Theological Education: "We cannot compromise on such basics as the study of Scripture and the Greek, the theology of the church, the history of the church, preaching, Christian education and leadership in worship. We must resist the temptation to water down basic curriculum by the addition of study after study that detracts from a certain essential core."

The only argument this observer would offer would be the first two years of theological education should be limited to Bible, theology, orthodox doctrine, history, and missions. A case can be made that in those theological seminaries that require an intern or vicarage year out between the second and last year of classroom study, a few electives could be offered to seniors from what is known as the practical field.

A second reason it is unrealistic and unreasonable to expect theological seminaries to teach leadership, strategies for change, evangelism, administration, or other "practical" courses is the context. The theological seminary classroom cannot be expected to provide the parish context needed for that kind of instruction.

A graduate school in a large research university can teach students about politics. It also may be able to teach students how to teach undergraduate courses on politics after they complete their doctorate and get a job in a four-year liberal arts college. That graduate school should not be expected to train students to become politicians! That is the responsibility of political parties, not of graduate schools.

The most that should be expected of theological seminaries in the so-called practical field is they might train students in the pedagogical skills required to teach other well-educated adults and to train students in basic communication skills including reading, writing, speaking, and preaching.

The other practical skills could best be taught in a two- or three- or four-year post-graduate residency on the staff of a large seven-day-a-week program church.

The third, and perhaps the most obvious reason theological seminaries should not be expected to offer a variety of courses in practical skills is that this simply adds to what already are excessive expectations.

Place the responsibility for offering those learning opportunities where it can best be accomplished—in that rapidly growing number of megachurches that have accepted this teaching role, in parachurch organizations, in teaching hospitals and mental health clinics, in governmental internships, in various denominational agencies, in the centers for teaching practical skills attached to dozens of large research universities, in professional schools, and in retreat centers. Reduce the expectations placed on theological seminaries to what they do best!

Finally, for the benefit of those who are reading this page in a bookstore while they contemplate spending the money required to purchase the book, a word needs to be said about the contents.

Why are some leaders more successful than others in rallying support for the implementation of new ideas? The predictable temptation is to answer that question by comparing the skills of the effective agent of planned change initiated from within an organization with the skills of the less successful leader. That may explain the difference. That explanation, however, often overlooks a critical variable. This is the context or environment for planned change. That environment is the theme of the first two chapters of this book. Neglecting the power of that context or climate can lead to frustration, disappointment, and rejection.

The crucial issue in this discussion is the vast difference between high commitment covenant communities and voluntary associations.

A brief third chapter introduces the fundamental point that planned change always begins with discontent with the status quo.

A society filled with people who contend one idea is as meritorious as another often challenges the advocates of planned change on the basis of authority. The fourth chapter reviews the shifting sources of authority. It emphasizes that for most of us in today's world, only rarely does adequate authority come with the office or title. It must be earned!

The fifth chapter underscores the thesis that leaders must lead. That means the advocate of change must be willing to initiate, to lead, and to decide.

Those seeking "nuts-and-bolts" suggestions on how to do it will find these in chapters six and eight. Both chapters lift up checklists on change for those who seek point-by-point checklists.

Between these chapters is an essay reflecting on what is the toughest question for aggressive and impatient advocates of change. Do I seek reform from within? Or do I take the easier and more promising choice of leaving and creating the new? The younger the reader, the more likely you will be motivated by the vision of a new tomorrow rather than by institutional loyalties.

Do not give up prematurely, perhaps the most productive beginning point will be to change the climate for change.

Chapter One

Covenant Community or Voluntary Association?

A couple of weeks after I moved here as your new pastor, I went out and spent three hours with the minister who has organized that five-year-old independent church on the north side of town," reflected the forty-one-year-old minister who had arrived seven months earlier as the senior pastor of the 658-member First Church. "I think you all know whom I'm talking about. They meet in a big steel building with a stone front near the intersection of highway 30 and the interstate. It turned out I was the first pastor ever to make an appointment to come out to see him, and he was unbelievably friendly. I soon found out why he is attracting so many new members. He represents the textbook definition of an ideological leader. To become a member of his congregation, you have to subscribe to an inerrant view of Scripture; you must accept as a factual account of history that Adam and Eve were the first human beings on earth; you must affirm every miracle described in the Bible; you must believe in heaven and hell; you must return to the Lord his tithe via that church; you must be a regular attender; and you must testify to a personal conversion experience that can be identified by when and where it occurred."

"I know the church and the minister," interrupted a fifty-six-year-old member of the governing board at First Church. "Our daughter and her husband are members of that congregation. It is clearly an extremely fundamentalist church. My wife and I have worshiped there twice. Neither of us is comfortable with that minister's theological position or with their music, but you have to give him credit for one thing. When you walk out, you know what he believes! Folks who are looking for certainty in their religious journey can find it there. My wife and I are more comfortable with ambiguity than are our daughter and son-in-law. That's why they go there and we come here. You also have to give that minister credit for being able to build a big congregation in only a few years. My understanding is they run between five and six hundred on Sunday morning and close to that on Sunday evening."

"This is all very interesting," observed Otto Bohn, a respected member of the governing board, "but I haven't the faintest idea of the relevance to what we have been discussing. We were talking about whether we should change our Sunday morning schedule from Sunday school followed by worship to a new schedule with two different worship services, one at eight-thirty and one at eleven. We now average about 350 to 375 at Sunday morning worship in a sanctuary that was designed to seat five hundred in the pews, two hundred in the balcony, and sixty in the choir. That means that on most Sundays, the room is half empty. When I joined this church forty years ago, we had only the one service on Sunday morning, and we always filled the pews and had people in the balcony. So, I am suggesting that we postpone talking about two services until we average at least 500 or more at worship. Now, all of a sudden we're talking about some fundamentalist church I know nothing about and care even less about. What's the point?"

"The point I was about to make was in response to Terry's suggestion that we just go ahead and introduce the new schedule on the second Sunday in September. After six months we will be able to evaluate the results and see if we want to continue with it or go back to the present schedule," patiently explained the pastor. "Terry's suggestion assumes some things about decision making that may or may not be valid here. I'm too new to know, but I want to raise them with you."

"Please go ahead and state your question," encouraged a veteran member. "What is the assumption you are questioning?"

"The point I was about to make is that there is a big difference in how you make decisions in a homogeneous movement or covenant community built around an ideological leader and what is appropriate in a long established organization that must be sensitive to generational differences. The pastor of that independent church is operating in a completely different context than I am here. He founded that congregation. He has seniority over every one of today's members. To a substantial degree he has built that congregation around the combination of his own belief system and his personality. It is still a movement led by an ideological leader. Any new idea or any proposal for change there has to meet only two tests. Is it consistent with the ideological position of that movement? Does it have the support of that pastor? If it passes those two tests, it is acceptable."

"That's the way they operate out there," confirmed the father of the daughter who was a member of that congregation. "If the minister wants it to happen and if the elders believe it is consistent with their ideological stance, that is all the approval needed. That is an elder-run church, and the minister is the number-one elder. They never ask the congregation to vote on anything. The members have two choices, comply or leave.

"By contrast," continued this recently arrived pastor, "this is a 119-year-old church with a system of self-government that places the ultimate control with the 658 people on our membership roll. This congregation called me to be the new senior minister. The members elected you to serve as their representatives on this governing board. We are accountable to the membership This other church is a covenant community or movement led by an ideological leader who also is the founding pastor. The founding pastor of this congregation has been dead for nearly a hundred years. He is still revered by a few, but he no longer is influential here. This is a mature organization, not an ideological movement or a covenant community."

"So, what does that have to do with our Sunday morning schedule?" challenged the impatient Otto Bohn.

"I still don't see why we can't go ahead and adopt a new schedule beginning in September and see how people respond to it," added Terry Winslow.

"We could, if we were an ideological movement or a covenant community," replied the pastor, "but we're not. This is a long established organization with lots of local traditions. Please do not misunderstand me. I support the proposed new schedule. That is not the point, however. The issue I'm concerned about is that we make that decision in a way that will be least disruptive. I'm not sure what is the best way to do that. It already is clear that Otto is not the only one here this evening who has reservations about changing the schedule, but I also know several other people who strongly favor the status quo."

Covenant Community Versus Voluntary Association

This pastor was wise to point out to the other members of the governing board of this twelve-decade-old congregation that it is a radically different institution from the new movement founded by an ideological leader. Whether or not that constitutes a useful beginning point for introducing a proposal to revise the Sunday morning schedule will be discussed in chapter 8. Six of these differences influence how proposals for change are introduced and adopted.

What Are the Cohesive Forces?

Perhaps the most obvious is that new independent congregation resembles a high commitment covenant community of people called together by an ideological leader to pioneer the creation of a new worshiping community. The cohesive forces that hold together that growing collection of people include (1) a clearly stated and widely shared belief system including theology and an approach to biblical interpretation, (2) the founding pastor is still the number-one leader, (3) the unifying goal of pioneering a new worshiping community, (4) the absence of local traditions or denominational requirements that could create diversionary struggles, (5) a high level of religious commitment, (6) the absence of a legalistic decision-making structure—trust in people, rather than a reliance on institutional safeguards to control the exercise of power, (7) a set of highly visible, specific, attainable, measurable, and unifying goals in creating that new worshiping community and in planning, financing, and constructing "our new church home," (8) a powerful and optimistic future orientation, (9) a central emphasis on world-wide missions, (10) to an increasing degree, friendship and kinship ties, and (11) a superior teaching ministry.[1]

Those eleven cohesive forces combine to provide a supportive environment for the introduction, adoption, and implementation of new ideas.

By contrast, the institutional environment at the 119-year-old First Church, which peaked in size twenty-two years ago with an average attendance of 570 in worship and 420 in the Sunday school, is not friendly toward new ideas. What are the cohesive forces holding that collection of people together today? High on that list are (1) long-time friendship ties; (2) habit; (3) institutional loyalties to that congregation and, for many of the long-time members, to that denomination; (4) an excellent ministry of music; (5) kinship ties; (6) local traditions and shared experiences out of the past; (7) affection for the former senior pastor who, after a thirty-five-year pastorate, retired two years ago, and his wife who continue to be regular attenders and who are both enthusiastic supporters of the new senior minister; (8) a widely shared affection for that building, which is filled with sacred memories for many of the long-time members; (9) five closely knit and long-lived adult Sunday school classes, the newest of which was organized six years ago; and (10) a powerful past-orientation.[2] A high level of religious commitment does not make that list when one-half of the members are absent from the corporate worship of God on the typical Sunday.

What began as a new worshiping community 119 years ago, organized around the proclamation of God's word, the proper administration of the sacraments, and the widely shared desire to create a community of believers who adhered to the same belief system, gradually has evolved into a voluntary association. Most of those ten contemporary cohesive forces reflect personal and social needs more than a response to a purely religious agenda.

Those ten cohesive forces have created an institutional environment that is more supportive of the status quo than change. It is an environment in which creativity is overshadowed by tradition and precedent. Change is more likely to be viewed as a threat rather than as a challenge.

Trust or Consensus?

On April 19, 1989, 500 pounds of propellant exploded in the center gun of turret two on the *USS Iowa*. This battleship had been brought out of mothballs five years earlier as part of a larger plan to expand the United States Navy. One of the dead sailors was named as the prime suspect who had planted a device that killed himself and 46 of his comrades.

This scapegoating of an enlisted man subsequently was publicly repudiated by Admiral Frank B. Kelso II. The classic definition of accountability in the Ameican Navy has always held the chain of command responsible for the safety and well-being of the crew. The commander of the ship is responsible for everything that happens on board that vessel. That is where the buck stops—at the commander's desk. It was both a violation of naval tradition and wrong to attempt to pass the buck to a young enlisted man. The key dynamic in decision making is trust.

A parallel structure can be found in many rapidly growing new missions. It also can be found in scores of large, long-established, complex, and numerically growing congregations. In these churches the founding pastor or the senior minister has earned the trust of the people. That minister understands that trust is based on a combination of the personal integrity of that pastor, competence, and a clear understanding that all decisions will be made for the benefit of that worshiping community, not for the self-aggrandizement or personal benefit or ego fulfillment of the pastor. That level of trust means the buck stops at the pastor's desk. (Sometimes this trust of the pastor as the leader of that institution is confused with the personal popularity of a minister. Personal popularity wins friends. Competence, commitment, integrity, character, and good judgment earn trust.) Except for the founding pastor of a new and fast-growing mission, that level of trust usually requires years to create. It does not automatically go with the office.

Ministers exercising this style of leadership can be found in congregations across the entire theological spectrum from liberal to fundamentalist. It is not a function of polity or theology. These ministers intuitively know the boundaries of their authority. Once they step over that line and demonstrate by their actions that their judgment or character is flawed, that trust evaporates. A sincere apology for "my mistake" does not restore the trust.

Sometimes a strong level of trust can be reestablished with a cadre of new leaders who were not present when that earlier slip in judgment occurred, but the long-time members and the veteran ex-leaders usually continue to withhold their unreserved trust in what they perceive to be a flawed leader. Sometimes the error in judgment is forgiven, but forgiveness does not automatically restore trust. Many volunteer leaders will forgive an isolated incident of poor judgment, but if that one incident turns into a pattern, forgiveness cannot recreate trust.

It also must be added that while good character and personal integrity do not guarantee competence in ministry, the absence of character can undermine what otherwise could be competent and trusted leadership.

The decision-making process in that new and large independent church described earlier shares one crucial parallel with the respected commander of a naval vessel. That is earned trust. Thus when the time came for that independent church to expand the schedule to two services on Sunday morning, the change was introduced with these words from the founding pastor. "Beginning with the first Sunday of next month, we will go to two services. Anyone who would like to participate in deciding on the exact schedule is invited to come to the meeting that will be held in the fellowship hall this Thursday evening at seven o'clock. We are especially interested in hearing from members of the choir, that is why we are scheduling this just before choir rehearsal, from teachers in the Sunday school, ushers, greeters, and anyone else. The crucial decision is whether we schedule the first service for 8:00 or 8:15 or 8:30 Sunday morning. The schedule of the National Football League requires the benediction for the second service be pronounced before twelve o'clock noon, so the maximum time we have to work with is four hours."

A completely different environment for making changes confronted the recently arrived senior minister at the 119-year-old First Church. What had begun as a covenant community gradually had evolved into a voluntary organization. That means it will be necessary to build a consensus, or at least an overwhelming majority in support of that proposal to revise the Sunday morning schedule. That minister is too new on the scene to have had the opportunity to earn the level of trust required for change to be accepted simply by an edict from the pastor.

Edict or Process?

From the perspective of a strategy for planned change, the critical difference between the high commitment covenant community and the voluntary association is the possibility of members withdrawing. The covenant community functions on the assumption that every member is completely committed to the ideals, purpose, belief system, and goals of that movement. That commitment eliminates the option of withdrawal.

By contrast, a central component of the definition of a voluntary association is every member retains the right of withdrawal. This means the decision-making process must function in a manner that minimizes the temptation to withdraw.

One product of this distinction is that decisions can be handed down by the leaders in a high commitment covenant community. The members have two choices. Comply or withdraw. Their deep commitment to that covenant community means that for most, the option of withdrawal is unthinkable. Therefore they comply.

By contrast, the wise leaders of what is clearly a voluntary association do not hand down edicts. They engage in a longer, far more complex, and difficult process of building support for the proposed change. This often means that in the high commitment covenant community, a decision is announced by the duly authorized leader(s). This assumes the support necessary for implementation will follow.

In the self-identified voluntary association, however, the process is reversed. Support for change is mobilized before any formal decision is made. (This process is described in detail in chapter 6.)

This distinction is not as sharp and clear as it first appears. Many congregations and denominations (and political parties and labor unions) that were created as movements have evolved into voluntary associations. The passage of time eroded many of those cohesive ties. Examples include the dilution of that common heritage in music; the decreasing proportion of members who enrolled in a Christian school that represented that covenant community; pluralistic views on doctrine and biblical interpretation; a reduced emphasis on home missions; interfaith and interdenominational marriages; the loss of a common Sunday school heritage; the erosion of denominational loyalties; decreased attendance at those huge annual celebrations, festivals, and conferences; the competition of other causes for the individual's time, energy, money, and loyalty; a lowering of the priority on world missions; the introduction of a variety of approved liturgies; the erosion of the power of kinship ties; and a drop in the quality of authorized leadership.

Thus, as one result, many decision-making procedures, which once were appropriate for a high commitment covenant community, are not working well today. As a denomination or congregation evolves into a voluntary association, the right of withdrawal becomes an acceptable, sometimes an even attractive option.

One example consists of the women who left the Christian Reformed Church back in the 1980s and 1990s because of the refusal of that body to ordain women. As long as everyone agreed that the denomination was a covenant community, they could continue to refuse to ordain women and only a small number of dissenters left. For the other dissenters, that option was not on their list of alternatives.

A second example is that huge number of younger third and fourth generation Roman Catholics who have left that church rather than comply with decisions from the hierarchy in birth control, celibacy, abortion, and the role of women. Their grandparents did not see withdrawal as an option.

A third example is the system of ministerial placement in The United Methodist Church. As long as the clergy viewed this as a brotherhood of ministers, or as a covenant community, they went where sent. The bishops could make appointments and expect that compliance and support would be forthcoming.

This system of ministerial placement has been undermined at many points. One has been the increasing number of lay leaders who view the church as a voluntary association and find the ministerial placement system to be incompatible with that perception of reality. That is one factor behind the aging of the membership of this denomination. The older members are not able to withdraw because of the cohesive ties that bind them to a particular congregation. The younger members find it easier to withdraw rather than comply.

A second factor was the decision to affirm pluralism. Pluralism is a compatible concept in a voluntary association, but not in a covenant community.

A third and perhaps the most influential factor has been the increasing number of the younger clergy who view their relationships with the other ministers in that annual conference as a voluntary association, not as a covenant community. The most highly visible evidence of this is the shrinking number of ministers who attend the memorial service for a deceased colleague. A less visible, but more significant symbol of this change is a sharp increase in the number of pastors who withdraw from the system after their second appointment. A third symbol of this change is in the growing number who choose early retirement.

A fourth factor has been the increasing number of pastors who are caught in a conflict of loyalties. Is my primary loyalty to my spouse? Or to this covenant community called an annual conference? Our changing society has made it difficult to place both of these loyalties at the top of the list.

A fifth factor undermining ministerial placement is that this no longer is the high commitment church it was in 1795 or 1815 or 1885 or even as recently as 1955. The increasing difficulty encountered in raising money for denominational agencies is but one of many signs of this drop in commitment. Designated giving often is opposed by leaders of the self-identified high commitment covenant community, but it is an effective tool in the voluntary association.

Finally, the gradual emergence of an adversarial relationship between many congregational leaders, who perceive the denomination as "the enemy," and the annual conference has undercut the trust level required to make the appointment system an acceptable method of ministerial placement.

Who Is the Client?

A fourth perspective for understanding the differences between the two congregations described earlier can be seen by looking at the origins and content of that proposed new schedule at First Church. Shortly after that beloved senior minister announced his impending retirement for reasons of health and age, the members of the worship committee met with members of the evangelism committee. A few years earlier someone had proposed a new schedule calling for two different worship experiences every Sunday morning. The goal was to reach a larger number of younger adults. This was quashed within the worship committee because of the strain it might place on this aging pastor who was in less than the best of health.

With the announcement of his retirement, members of these two committees agreed that the time was coming to resurrect their plan. The newly arrived senior minister was invited to become a full participant in designing the proposed schedule and strongly affirmed the goal of reaching and serving a younger generation of adults.

Thus the fourth big difference between these two congregations is discerned because that new independent congregation was organized around the primary goal of saving souls. Any proposal for a revised Sunday morning schedule probably would win quick approval if it promised to expand the evangelistic outreach. For those leaders the number-one client is still the unchurched population.

Back at First Church, however, the definition of the client is more complicated. When the revised schedule was first considered, the number-one client was perceived to be the aging senior minister. That revision was rejected on the assumption that the new schedule would place an excessive work load on the pastor.

Some of the proponents of the new schedule saw this aging and shrinking congregation as the number-one client. They believed the time had come to reverse that pattern of numerical decline by attracting more younger new members. Others saw the new senior minister as the number-one client. If the new pastor did not endorse it, the new schedule probably was dead in the water.

At least a few saw the number-one client to be the existing membership in general and the governing board in particular. This group included Terry Winslow who was eager to adopt the new schedule and "let it sell itself." Terry was convinced if the potential opponents saw a large number of younger adults flocking to that proposed new earlier service before Sunday school, they would enthusiastically endorse it.

A couple of Terry's allies agreed the most urgent need was to minimize any possible opposition from the traditionalists. That was the explanation they offered for simply adding a new and different service at 8:30 A.M. Sunday. This would not disturb the existing schedule for Sunday school at nine-thirty followed by worship at eleven.

The moral of this story is the larger the number and variety of clients, the more difficult it is to win support for implementing any one specific proposal for change. Each client has a somewhat different agenda.

If the number-one client had been perceived to be younger adults who were not actively involved in any worshiping community, a different process might have been followed. This could have involved bringing together three dozen younger adults. Some would have been completely unchurched people. Others might have been younger adults who were members of First Church, plus their friends who rarely attended church on Sunday morning. A few might have been the adult children of members who lived in this community but were not regular church-goers.

This collection of younger adults could have been enlisted by either the retiring or the new senior pastor, or by the associate minister, to constitute the general planning committee to create that new worship experience. Seven of them could have been asked to design the worship experience for that first weekend.

Seven others could have been asked to create a vocal choir or to organize an instrumental group. Another seven could have been placed in charge of publicity. Seven others could have been asked to serve as greeters, ushers, and liturgists. Seven could have been given the responsibility for refreshments and the fellowship period following worship.

This general committee could have decided whether they preferred Saturday evening or Sunday morning. They also could have negotiated with the governing board on the hour and the place. With three dozen young adults actively involved in planning that first service, a reasonable goal would have been an attendance of between 60 and 600 by the fifth week.

The process described here resembles the creation of a new movement and would be based on the dynamics of a movement. A central part of that process is to begin with a definition of the needs of the people to be served. They represent the number-one client. That is a radically different approach to planned change than beginning with the needs of a long established organization and working within the permission-granting and permission-withholding boundaries of that organization.

The fact that young adults were not the number-one client at First Church introduces a fifth perspective for reflecting on the differing environments for change between a relatively new covenant community with an ideological leader and an aging voluntary organization.

Past or Future Orientation?

Why do old men enjoy sitting out in the sun and reminiscing about the past while young men prefer to talk with one another about their dreams for the future?

One reason is that those old men have a rich storehouse of memories accumulated over many years. Their lives are largely behind them. When one of the group dies, the survivors talk about his past. By contrast, most of the young men anticipate a future that will be more attractive than their past. When one of those young men is killed in an accident or in a war, the survivors talk about the future he did not live to see and enjoy.

Why do organizations that have drifted away from their original purpose continue to survive and maintain the support necessary to survive? The organizational landscape is cluttered with voluntary associations that no longer focus on their original purpose of wiping out polio or operating homes for orphans or converting Native Americans or caring for unwed mothers or sheltering newcomers to the city or caring for recent immigrants or countless other purposes.

They survive, in part because they created a closely knit group of committed supporters who derive great satisfactions from a collection of deeply meaningful, shared experiences. A second reason may be that the gathering place has become an important "third place" (in addition to their places of residence and their places of work) that affirms their personal identity as human beings.[3] Another reason may be this organization affirms and supports some deeply held cultural values that are threatened by the changing world in which they now live.

These four paragraphs introduce a common, but less than universal, distinction between ideologically based social movements or covenant communities and aging voluntary associations. The first display a powerful future orientation as they seek to change the world. The key central unifying principles usually are (1) discontent with the status quo, (2) an ideologically driven leader, and (3) a cause that becomes the rallying point for enlisting new recruits. This common pattern can be found in the lives of St. Paul, Martin Luther, John Wesley, Martin Luther King, Jr., and many other reformers.

In other words, social movements are organized around discontinuity with the status quo and a desire to influence the shape of tomorrow.

By contrast, the aging voluntary association often displays a powerful past orientation, places a high value on tradition, and affirms the importance of friendship ties and shared experiences from the past. As what once were future-oriented and high commitment social movements organized around a shared vision of a new tomorrow gradually evolve into aging voluntary associations, the past becomes longer and more influential. When a new vision of a new tomorrow conflicts with the sacred traditions of the past, it becomes easy to rally people to resist change and to seek to perpetuate yesterday. The new social movement naturally is receptive to change. The aging voluntary association naturally resists change.

Charisma or Goals?

For this next discussion, we can divide the world into three parts. One is the relatively new congregation that functions like an ideologically centered social movement. The independent church referred to earlier illustrates that facet of reality. The second is the organization that currently enjoys the leadership of a creative, enthusiastic, and charismatic individual who has earned the unreserved trust and confidence of all the volunteer leaders. Those situations are exempt from all the standard rules for initiating and implementing change. The third part of this scenario includes the vast majority of ecclesiastical organizations, both congregations and denominational agencies. Most of them respond in a normal and predictable manner when confronted with proposals for change.

How would one introduce a proposal to revise the Sunday morning schedule in each of these situations?

The founding pastor in the new mission points out that this is a good way to proclaim to more peeople the good news that Jesus Christ is Lord and Savior. This assertion probably will be sufficient to overcome any objection that might be raised.

The respected and charismatic leader intuitively foresees the best time to suggest going to two services. The new schedule wins approval partly on the basis of logic, but largely on that wave of earned trust engendered by the personality, judgment, character, integrity, and performance of that leader.

In the long-established congregation—with a strong past orientation, a preference for perpetuating the status quo, a love of continuity, a fear of discontinuity, and tremendous respect for tradition—life is more complicated.

In this situation, the person(s) seeking to expand the number and variety of worship experiences will be well advised to recognize (1) that proposal has many clients, (2) no one argument will persuade everyone to support the change, (3) most normal people need time to talk themselves into accepting a new way of life (that is one reason God made the time between conception and the birth of a new baby nine months, not nine hours or nine days or nine weeks), (4) the definition of self-interest is not the same for everyone, (5) rarely do people endorse what they perceive to be a radical departure from the status quo unless they also are convinced of a pressing need to change (no one can teach an adult anything that adult does not want to learn), (6) it is always wise to err on the side of winning excessive support rather than to err on the side of asking for a decision with too little support, and (7) the only safe assumption is the immediate, natural, and normal response of every individual will be to reject any and all proposals for change in favor of perpetuating the status quo.

How does one introduce change into this resistance? One answer is to seek the charismatic leader who is able to win surprising support for what many perceive to be radical ideas. Given the contemporary shortage of charismatic leaders in both congregational and denominational circles, what is the next best course of action? For many other leaders, that means creating an environment that is supportive of creativity, innovation, and change. That raises an issue that deserves a chapter by itself.

Chapter Two

What Is the Climate?

What is the environment for change in your congregation? In your denomination? Is that setting open to and supportive of creativity, new ideas, and innovation? Or is it hostile to change? Five different scenarios will illustrate the range of possibilities. This is not an exhaustive list but intended only for self-evaluation purposes. After you have identified where your congregation or denomination fits on this spectrum, it will be easier to outline an action plan for creating a more supportive environment. Please note that it is rare for all members of a congregation or denominational family to agree that any one of these five scenarios precisely and completely describes the local situation. Therefore the central question really is, What are the dominant characteristics of your environment or climate for change?

Is This an Adversarial Environment?

Unquestionably, the easiest of these to identify is the organization that is at least partially immobilized by adversarial relationships. The college or university president may be convinced that the faculty is the number-one obstacle to progress. Many of the faculty identify the president as the number-one enemy and at least a few are prepared to join the revolution designed to oust that leader.[1] In a regional judicatory the adversaries of the current president or bishop or chief executive may be actively organizing the campaign to defeat the incumbent at the next election or to force an early retirement. The recently elected trustee of a national board of a particular denomination or of the theological seminary may have sought that office in order to force the resignation of the chief executive officer. An adult Sunday school class organized many years earlier by a greatly beloved previous pastor around Bible study, fellowship, caring, and special events may change its agenda and place the removal of the present pastor at the top of the list of current priorities.

During the first several decades of this century, a widespread example of an adversarial environment was the conflict between the newly arrived pastor and the veteran Sunday school superintendent. That Sunday school superintendent may have celebrated the departure of three or four pastors, but eventually became the victim of that environment. (The guiding generalization is that only rarely does the part-time volunteer prevail over the competent full-time staff person who places a high priority on personal survival.)

It is not irrelevant to note that (a) this widespread conflict between the pastor and the leaders in the Sunday school appears to have been one of the more influential factors behind the 35 to 60 percent decline in Sunday school attendance between 1950 and 1990 and (b) the history of conflict is one reason that it is extremely important to enlist the pastor or the senior minister as an ally when seeking to expand the teaching ministry of your church.[2]

Ever since the days of President Dwight D. Eisenhower, it has not been uncommon for the adversarial relationships between the president's chief of staff and several cabinet members to immobilize that administration for several months.

Perhaps the most common expressions of adversarial relationships in the larger multiple staff congregations involve the recently arrived senior pastor and one or two inherited and long-tenured staff members who have a strong personal coterie of loyal supporters. Sometimes this is the minister of music, occasionally it is the church secretary or the director of Christian education. When it is the number-one associate minister who was an active candidate for the position of senior minister, but was rejected in favor of an outsider, the best resolution is the early submission of that associate minister's resignation.

In recent years the contacts between the leaders, both paid staff and volunteers, in many of the very large congregations and the regional or national agencies of that denomination have degenerated into an adversarial relationship. This usually is the product of either (a) a conflict over priorities and/or (b) the criteria guiding the selection of representatives for the board of that agency and/or (c) the criteria for selecting staff and/or (d) the failure of denominational staff to answer the mail and/or (e) adversarial relationships among the professional staff of that denominational agency and/or (f) the evolution of the primary role of the denomination from the resourcing of congregations into the care of the clergy or a redefinition into a role as a regulatory agency.[3]

In recent years that adversarial climate has spread to the public schools, to the internal administration of newspapers, to the relationships between residents and the officials of local government, and to residents of condominiums and cooperative apartment buildings. That climate also has created an unprecedented quantity of litigation and the continuous threat of lawsuits. About the only beneficiaries of this trend are attorneys and their office staffs.

At this point the impatient reader may ask, "So what?" The answer has three facets. First, it is exceptionally difficult to secure broad-based support for the implementation of any proposal for any change in an organization disrupted by adversarial relationships. Second, frequently the response is not acceptance and approval, but rather a compromise that evades the central motivating factor behind the proposal for change. Third, from a long-term perspective, the most productive course of action may be to postpone any proposals for change until after that internal conflict has been resolved.

Is Apathy Worse?

A sharply different environment is encountered when the climate is dominated by apathy. A common symptom is when nearly all of the worshipers, including the pastor, have departed from the building within five to ten minutes after the benediction has been pronounced. A second is when the majority of potential volunteers who are asked to accept a particular assignment refuse. A third is when a significant number of members of a particular committee or board rarely attend the scheduled meetings of that group. A crucial symptom is when the budget for the coming year is not even close to being fully underwritten in advance. The most serious symptom is when lay officials choose to worship elsewhere on Sunday morning.

In congregational life this condition also may be identified as passivity. When that turns out to be an accurate diagnosis, the first step is to activate that passive parish.[4] Sometimes this process will include efforts to rally support for overdue changes. More often the focus will be on redefining purpose, role, and goals. Without a reasonably broad-based agreement on purpose and role, it is nearly impossible, except in the midst of a widely perceived crisis, to formulate and implement meaningful goals.[5]

In recent years several denominations have experienced an era in which adversarial relationships dominated the life of that religious body. The Lutheran Church-Missouri Synod in the late 1960s and 1970s and the Southern Baptist Convention in the late 1970s and 1980s stand out as the two most widely publicized examples. A third came in the second half of 1991 in the Christian Church (Disciples of Christ) when that denomination's official nominating committee's candidate for the office of general minister and president failed to gain the majority necessary for election.[6] A fourth example of seriously divisive adversarial relationships within one denomination came in May 1992 at the General Conference of The United Methodist Church, when a motion to add the phrase *offer Christ as Savior* to a proposal for ministering to the needs of Native Americans was adopted by a vote of 503 to 441 and a proposal to move their global mission agency out of New York City was passed by a vote of 485 to 470.

Despite these and other highly publicized incidents, the dominant climate within the older mainline denominations no longer is marked by adversarial relationships. The current climate more closely resembles apathy. Unless an utterly outrageous proposal emerges from a denominational agency, most of the people in the pews, and a majority of parish pastors, shrug their shoulders and go about their business as a worshiping community.

A parallel response of apathy confronts those who seek to re-create the exciting denominationally based ecumenical coalitions of the 1960s. Interchurch coalitions today are largely congregationally based.

The adoption and implementation of most proposals for substantial change require broad-based discontent with the status quo. When apathy, rather than discontent, dominates that environment, it is difficult to arouse the support required to implement any proposed change.

Perhaps the most significant implication of this climate is that denominational goals or programs or special emphases no longer are effective as rallying points for congregations. One example is that proposals from denominational or ecumenical groups urging congregations to adopt a particular course of action or to financially support a specific project or to study the report of an ad hoc committee on a controversial issue rarely arouse an enthusiastic response. Most of these proposals drown in a sea of apathy. The more controversial are rejected by a wave of hostility.

While not highly important as an issue, an interesting symbol of this apathetic attitude by congregational leaders toward denominational headquarters can be found in the name of hundreds of new and relocated congregations. The denominational affiliation is not reflected in that name. In some cases the omission of the denominational label was motivated in part by the fact that the name of that particular denomination exceeds seven syllables. The ideal denominational name, if the expectation is that it will be incorporated into congregational names, will be three syllables or less. That will permit a name of five or seven syllables for each congregation. Examples include East Side Baptist Church, First Presbyterian Church, Trinity Lutheran

Church, First Methodist Church, and Central Church of God. The ideal name will be three or five syllables. If it is more than seven syllables, it is tempting to delete all or part of the denominational label.

When the relationship between the congregation and the denomination is marked by apathy, who cares whether the label of that religious tradition is carried in the name of that parish? Congregations can send money to denominational headquarters, but not back it up with a strong commitment to denominational goals.

Who Has a Voice?

A third environment, which is less widespread among the churches today than it was in the 1950s, is characterized by the fact that on every issue of any significance, the pastor often casts the majority of decisive votes. This is most common in Roman Catholic, United Methodist, and Episcopal parishes and in many African-American congregations. This decision-making environment also can be found in dozens of large and rapidly growing independent congregations, in many Lutheran parishes, and in a small proportion of Southern Baptist churches. It is rarest in Reformed and Presbyterian congregations.

"Whatever the pastor wants, the pastor gets," is a common refrain among the volunteer leaders, including some disenchanted, angry, alienated, and older ex-leaders who saw their power greatly eroded since the arrival of the current pastor. Some of the friendly and appreciative supporters describe the pastor as a "benevolent dictator." "I greatly prefer the benevolent dictator who gets things done to the passive minister who sits around waiting for others to take the initiative." That positive evaluation frequently is offered when the benevolent dictator arrived after years of congregational drift during the tenure of the self-identified "enabler" who combined incompetence with a total absence of initiative.

As a general pattern (1) the larger the congregation and/or (2) the more rapid the rate of numerical growth and/or (3) the more meaningful the worship experiences and/or (4) the newer the congregation and/or (5) the longer the tenure of the present senior minister and/or (6) the stronger the teaching ministry and/or (7) the greater the emphasis on worldwide missions, the more receptive the congregation will be to a pastor who comes in and "runs the whole show."

At the other end of the spectrum, a far less hospitable environment exists for the benevolent dictator when two or more of these conditions prevail: (1) the worship-attendance-to-confirmed membership ratio is below 80 percent, (2) the number of new members received annually by letter or certificate of transfer is fewer than five for every one hundred confirmed members, (3) at least one-third of all high-school-age members stay away from all youth programs, (4) the average attendance at Sunday morning worship is declining, (5) less than 30 percent of all member contributions are allocated to missions, (6) the predecessor who served as senior pastor for an extended period of time was greatly respected and highly effective and placed much of the control over important decisions in the hands of volunteer leaders, (7) the senior minister lacks the unreserved support of many of the full-time staff, (8) the music ministry is far less extensive than one would expect to find in a congregation of this size, and (9) the median age of the membership is rising.

With two significant exceptions, the presence of the benevolent dictator can be a productive environment for planned change. The obvious exception, of course, is that no significant changes are implemented unless they have the support of that senior minister. Perhaps a more serious reservation, however, is the benevolent dictator is far more acceptable to people born before 1945 than to those born after 1955. That is one part of the explanation for the sharply increased size of that parade of people reared in a Roman Catholic home who have left to join a Protestant congregation with a congregational polity. That generational difference also is one part of a more complicated explanation for the aging of the membership in The United Methodist Church mentioned in chapter 1.

What happens if the chief executive officer (bishop, conference minister, president, regional minister, presbytery executive, et al.) of the regional judicatory turns out to be a dictator? In 1955 the answer was considerable affirmation if the performance exceeded people's expectations. In 1970 the answer often was hostility and the emergence of an adversarial relation with the churches. In 1990 that leadership style by a denominational leader, either regional or national, was most likely to evoke considerable apathy and a passive ignoring of denominational pronouncements, programs, or goals.

Is Complacency the Issue?

For many proponents of planned change, apathy is only the second worst environment in which to function. The worst is excessive comfort with the status quo. This "earned complacency" most often surfaces following the successful outcome of what had been a stress-producing experience.

In one congregation a twenty-five-year pastorate came to an end five or six years after it should have been terminated. The last five years of what had been an effective pastorate were filled with anger, frustration, disappointments, numerical decline, internal conflict, and the reluctant resignations of two valuable long-time staff members. Eighteen months later, the members were rejoicing following the arrival of an exceptionally competent, deeply committed, and remarkably personable young pastor who appeared to be the perfect match for that parish's needs. To everyone's surprise and delight, the two other replacement staff members surpassed their predecessors in professional and interpersonal skills. The internal tension had been replaced by a flood of euphoria. "Everything is perfect here just the way it is, let's not change a thing."

A thousand miles away, a small rural congregation meeting in a ninety-year-old building located on a one-acre parcel of land, most of which was used by the cemetery, saw that sacred meeting place destroyed by fire. The county would not issue a building permit for a new structure unless they acquired more land so no one would park on the narrow road on which the church was located. The farmer who owned the surrounding land was still embroiled in a thirty-year feud with the two most influential member families over the congregation's refusal to allow his parents to be buried in that cemetery. Finally, with great reluctance, the congregation (1) incorporated a separate cemetery association that took control of the old site, (2) purchased a five acre site two miles east at the intersection of a state highway and a county road, (3) raised $100,000 to go with the money received from the insurance company and constructed a highly attractive and functional 5,500-square-feet meeting place, (4) paved a parking lot that would accommodate sixty vehicles, and (5) paid the last bill on the entire effort a week before they occupied the new building. This congregation was and is served by a gregarious, competent, and caring pastor who also serves a larger congregation meeting in a building seven miles south. That pastor lived in a deteriorated parsonage next to that church building. As a "bonus" the committee at the smaller congregation constructed a 2,000-square-feet parsonage on that five-acre site and invited the pastor to live there. The other congregation cheerfully agreed. This was more attractive than spending $15,000 to renovate the old parsonage on their site. Today that rural congregation enjoys an excellent meeting place on an attractive site with plenty of convenient and safe parking, a net gain of two or three members annually, the leadership of a competent and personable resident pastor, and the immense satisfactions of a miraculous recovery from what had been first perceived as a great disaster. Who would want to change that scenario?

While the local circumstances are never identical, thousands of congregations enjoy an earned complacency that is highly supportive of the status quo. Among the more common characteristics of these congregations are these: (1) a balanced budget that allocates a respectable proportion for missions; (2) a full complement of standing committees staffed by dedicated members who carry out their basic responsibilities in a satisfactory manner; (3) a good match exists between pastor and parish; (4) the members enjoy a satisfactory meeting place; (5) the number of adults received as new members annually matches or exceeds the number of losses; (6) local precedents are highly influential in decision making; (7) long tenure receives the deserved

respect; (8) the Sunday morning schedule is relatively uncompli-
cated; (9) a point of local pride is the absence of discontent,
petty complaints, bickering, or griping; (10) the members share
an appreciation for continuity with the past; (11) excellent pastoral care is provided to the members; (12) worship and preaching is at or above an acceptable level; (13) members brag about
their attractive Sunday school; and (14) an above average quality
organizational life (Sunday school, women's fellowship, choir,
youth group, and, perhaps, a men's group) provides comfortable stability zones within that larger fellowship.

One reason these congregations tend to be complacent is they
have much to be complacent about when compared to other
churches. The mood is characterized by the slogan, "Don't fix
what ain't broke."

The response to a proposal for change parallels what happens
when the sixty-five-year-old husband returns from his annual
physical examination. The physician concluded the examination
by declaring, "You're in about the same shape you were in when
I first examined you nine years ago, except you're nine years
older." On sharing that evaluation with his wife, he is told, "If
you ask me, I think you would be better off if you went on a diet
and lost fifteen or twenty pounds." What are the chances that
husband will eagerly accept the challenge to go on a diet? What
are the chances the complacent congregation will enthusiastically welcome proposals to alter the status quo?

Is This a Supportive Environment?

What is one of the most common characteristics of a congregation that is experiencing a gradual decrease in numbers? During the past decade the average attendance in Sunday school is
down 25 percent, worship attendance has dropped by 20 percent, after adjusting for inflation, member contributions are
down 15 percent, and the high school youth group has 35 percent fewer teenagers involved on a regular basis.

What is the response out of denominational headquarters
·when the total membership is dropping by one-half of one per-

cent annually, dollar receipts from congregations are decreasing by 3 percent annually after adjustments for inflation, when the number of professional staff has to be reduced year after year, and when the financial squeeze means a reduction in the number of new congregations launched each year?

The widely expected answer in both scenarios is an openness to creativity, innovation, new ideas, and change. That is a natural, predictable, naive, and unrealistic hope.

In real life, in both scenarios, institutional survival goals take over the agenda. That emphasis on survival often creates a tenacious desire to maintain the status quo or, better yet, to recreate yesterday. This tends to be a more predictable pattern in congregations than in denominational circles.

At denominational headquarters a common temptation is to change the agenda. The new agenda may be a proposal to restructure or to relocate the headquarters or to merge with another denomination or to focus on social, economic, and political issues or to emphasize the globalization of the church or to embark on a capital funds appeal or to redefine our definition of missions or to schedule a huge national convocation designed to raise morale, deepen loyalties to that denomination, and produce a memorable shared experience for those in attendance. (This last can be a productive course of action if at least 5 to 10 percent of the total membership attends.) The predictable congregational response is an increase in the level of apathy.

The congregational response to those shrinking numbers may lead to a proposal to renovate the meeting place or to spend more time on Sunday morning exhorting members to contribute more money or to a reduction in the size of the staff or to budget more money for bigger ads in the local newspaper or to have more congregational dinners or to reduce the financial support for missions or to seek rent-paying tenants for empty space in the building or to build a new parsonage for the minister or to encourage the pastor to seek a Doctor of Ministry degree or to cut back on the Sunday morning schedule from two worship services to one or to merge two shrinking circles in the women's organization or two adult classes in the Sunday school or to operate a cooperative vacation Bible school with one or two other congregations or to join with two other churches in a union Thanksgiving or Good Friday service or to cut back on the summer schedule to give both Sunday school teachers and choir members a longer vacation or to combine Sunday school and worship at the same hour in hopes this will attract families with young children or to plan a big celebration of the twenty-fifth anniversary of the pastor's ordination.

Now, having written all the positive endorsements this observer can think of about each of those alternatives, let us move on to the central issue.

In voluntary asssociations, the number-one characteristic that is supportive of proposals for change is numerical growth. Numerically growing movements and organizations (1) rarely give a high priority to institutional survival goals; (2) are exceptionally open to new ideas and innovation; (3) provide a high level of tolerance for and occasionally even affirm the maverick personality; (4) usually respond enthusiastically to big challenges; (5) enjoy surprises; (6) display a strong and positive future orientation; (7) support leaders who often color outside the lines; (8) are comfortable with discontinuity with the past; (9) by definition, since they are numerically growing organizations, display an above average sensitivity to the needs of outsiders and are able to offer meaningful responses to those needs; (10) are at least as comfortable with the new as with the traditional; (11) are able to give serious consideration to proposals for change without being threatened or feeling their past performance is being challenged; and (12) tend to be able to attract and keep paid staff members who display a far above average level of professional competence. Those generalizations apply to both congregations and denominations as well as parachurch organizations and other voluntary associations.

Two important lessons emerge from this set of observations. First, if you are a leader in a numerically growing denomination, congregation, or parachurch organization, you probably enjoy a favorable environment for creativity, new ideas, innovation, and change.

Second, and for many readers this is more relevant, if you are a leader in a numerically declining organization, a high priority should be given to creating a more supportive local climate for innovation and change.

If Not, What Do We Do Next?

The supportive environment for change shares several characteristics with the complacent organization, but the differences are more significant than the similarities. The number-one difference, if it exists, already has been identified. The complacent organization usually is on a plateau in size while the most hospitable environments are found in numerically growing movements and organizations.

If the agenda calls for introducing changes into a complacent or apathetic organization, the first requirement of the leader is to recognize this will not be easy. The second step is to understand the merits of patience, persistence, redundant internal communication, and skilled leadership plus the value of allies. (See chapter 3.) The third step is to improve the environment to make it more supportive of change. If apathy or complacency dominate that environment, the next step is to transform that environment. After that effort is well underway, consideration can be given to introducing proposals for change.

A review of how the environment for change in apathetic or complacent congregations was changed to make it more supportive reveals eight common components. The first is to improve the quality of pastoral care. This goes beyond the care of people with problems. The critical component is giving people the opportunity to be heard and to know they are being heard. In smaller congregations the pastor usually accomplishes this by two or three visits in every household annually. In middle-sized churches annual visits are combined with a variety of group experiences. Cottage meetings, hearings, and dinners are scheduled. In larger parishes this system normally requires enlisting and training a cadre of volunteers who complete three calls on each household on their list.[7]

Concurrently, a second step to offer every member who feels the need for it participation in a small-to-middle-sized group in which continuity, stability, predictability, fellowship, and mutual support are among the dominant characteristics. Examples of such groups include a circle in the women's organization (if the women's organization insists on rotating the membership in the circles every year or two, that policy usually undermines the effectiveness of the circles to serve as stability zones), one or more continuing adult Sunday school classes, the Tuesday Bible study group that has been in existence with largely the same membership for years, a prayer cell, the church softball team, perhaps the Christian education committee or any other board with long-tenured membership, the men's fellowship, the chancel choir, or the board of deacons. Most people are more open to change if they enjoy the comfort of what Alvin Toeffler described as personal stability zones. A personal stability zone is marked by enduring relationships with other people, continuity, predictability, and dependability.[8]

Occasionally, a leader will mistakenly identify these stability zones as nests of opposition to change. That may be true on the surface, but probably that is a result of the neglect of the members of these stability zones. The basic premise is that a healthy stability zone enables people to enjoy the challenge of change. A simple example is the person who travels extensively for a living is more likely to enjoy those new experiences if the traveler's home life is a healthy stability zone filled with enduring relationships.

A third ingredient in the process of transforming an apathetic or complacent congregation into a supportive environment for change is for the leader(s) to identify those strands of local traditions that can be affirmed and built on in planning for the future. This requires a reasonable degree of knowledge of local history and may go back to documents explaining why this congregation was founded. Thus a proposal to revise the Sunday morning schedule to strengthen the Sunday school may begin with the fact that this congregation traces its history back to 1907 when Old First Church established a Sunday school mission in this neighborhood. That mission subsequently evolved into this congregation. In another case the proposal for a million dollar capital funds campaign began with a reference to when this congregation raised $250,000 in 1968. After allowing for inflation, changes in per capita personal income and the size of the congregation, that effort would be equivalent to $1.6 million today—so the new proposal is relatively modest by comparison.

The fourth, and perhaps the most subtle of this transforming process is to introduce greater reliance on ad hoc study committees and ad hoc action committees. Standing committees tend to focus on continuity with the past, maintaining a traditional routine and extending yesterday into tomorrow. This also means standing committees usually attract as members people who are comfortable with the past, enjoy continuity, and tend to resist change.

By contrast, ad hoc study committees usually are more comfortable challenging the status quo, planning for a tomorrow that they believe will be different from yesterday, and ignoring local precedents. Ad hoc action committees tend to be more goal-oriented than standing committees and often are comfortable with what others perceive to be revolutionary changes.[9]

Perhaps the simplest illustration of these differences can be seen when irreconcilable differences surface between the minister and another staff member. If this conflict is referred to a standing committe on personnel, the predictable result is the members of that committee will seek to reconcile the differences. The minister and the staff member will be urged to pray about this, to talk to each other, perhaps to seek professional counseling, or to change their behavior patterns. It is not unusual for this mess to drag on for a year or two without resolution, despite eight or ten meetings of that standing committee.

If a special action committee is created to resolve this conflict, they may spend one meeting accepting the fact that this really is an irreconcilable conflict, a second meeting deciding which of the two people will be asked to resign, and a third meeting working out the terms of the termination arrangement.

The moral of this story is standing committees are comfortable with continuity with the past while ad hoc committees are more likely to be comfortable with change. Therefore, introduce the concept of task forces and ad hoc committees first with minor changes. Subsequently, when people have begun to accept this change in the organizational structure, create the new ad hoc committees to introduce radical change.

A fifth component is to identify the respected and influential volunteers who, when the time comes, can help to legitimatize new ideas. Rarely is it possible to persuade everyone to support a new idea simply by lifting up the merits of the proposed change. At least one-third, and perhaps two-thirds of the members will be influenced more by the opinions of these legitimatizers than they will by the contents of the proposed change.

A sixth component of this strategy to transform the environment usually is led by the pastor, but rarely can it be accomplished alone. This requires identifying and celebrating the victories however minor they may be. The addition of a couple of newcomers to the choir, a large turnout for a special event, an increase in the average attendance at worship, the service project completed by the youth group, the first time in many months that the treasurer reported a surplus in the bank account, the creation of a new circle in the women's organization, or the formation of a new Bible study group are examples of victories that should be lifted up and celebrated.

The goal is to create, on the basis of factual evidence, the impression among the people that "things are beginning to happen here" or "this place isn't dead after all" or "that's a piece of good news." Larger success stories often require the foundation of minor successes before anyone is willing to tackle the big challenge. Create the momentum that can help secure support for innovation.

The seventh component is one that is widely neglected. The basic generalization behind this is that (a) the larger the size of the congregation and/or (b) the weaker the group life and/or (c) the more complex the community setting and/or (d) the longer the journey from members' homes to church and/or (e) the longer that congregation has been in existence, the more likely the grapevine will do you more harm than good.

In other words, a crucial step is to create a reliable, accurate, redundant, and lucid system of internal communication. Bad news travels faster and further than good news! A substantial amount of potential opposition to change can be eliminated before it surfaces with high quality internal communication.

One of the keys is redundancy. This means sending the same message via several different channels. These channels may include announcements in the bulletin, posters, letters, telephone calls, face-to-face visits, radio, newspaper articles, videotapes, a parish newsletter, postcards, cottage meetings, the annual congregational meeting, bulletin boards, and announcements via groups in that congregation.

Another key to this process can be the parish newsletter if it is designed to be read by the recipient. Which newsletters are read by the recipients? Those that are filled with news about the members, stories about what is happening in that parish, plans for the future, and accounts of both personal and congregational victories.

Which newsletters are not read? Those that are filled with "oughts" and "shoulds," with exhortations about what the readers should do, with boring summaries of next Sunday's sermon (or worse yet, of last Sunday's sermon), with reflections on a trip by a staff member, with bad news about the finances, with the problems disturbing the pastor, and with reprints of notices from denominational headquarters.

An effective internal communication system is the key to the eighth ingredient in a supportive environment. This can be summarized in two words. No surprises! Long before any proposal for substantial change is presented for formal consideration, that proposal should be processed through the informal channels. Normally, this process begins, not with the proposal for change, but rather with enlarging the circle of discontent with the status quo. That discontent with the status quo provides a natural setting for the introduction of a variety of "solutions to our problem." Thus when a specific action proposal eventually is introduced, no one is surprised. That was one of the alternatives discussed earlier.

Another way of looking at this point is to remember an ancient bit of wisdom. Irrelevance is answering questions no one has asked. Proposals for change should never come as surprises. They should be presented as one of two more responses to discontent with the status quo. (See chapter 3.)

The second half of this point also can be summarized by another piece of ancient wisdom. The normal, natural, and predictable response to an unsolicited proposal for change is rejection. The best way to minimize the possibilities of rejection of this brilliant solution to a pressing problem is to avoid surprising people.

After the transformation of that congregational environment from apathetic or complacent to supportive for new ideas is well underway on all eight of the fronts described above, the initiator(s) of planned change can begin to spread the seeds of discontent with the status quo. When doing this, it is important to observe the distinction beween criticizing current leaders, members, or programs and challenging people to a more faithful and meaningful ministry. One way of doing this is to identify the discrepancy between what is and what could be. A better way is to create situations in which members can identify that discrepancy.

What About That Adversarial Climate?

A word needs to be added about the situation when the local climate is dominated by adversarial relationships. What can the self-identified agent of planned change do in those situations? One answer is, "Not much."

A second and better response is to identify a unifying goal that will win broad-based support and completely overshadow in importance the worst of those divisive issues. The number-one example of that in the United States came in late 1941. On December 3, 1941 this nation was badly divided over American foreign policy, the growing deficit of the federal government which had reached unprecedented proportions, what to do about unemployment, and a dozen other domestic issues. A week later, after the day that President Franklin D. Roosevelt had declared "would live in infamy," the nation was united around the single goal of defeating two enemies.

Congregational examples include the tornado that destroys the homes of a dozen parishioners, the fire that burns the church building to the ground, the shattering announcement that the cheerful thirty-seven-year-old spouse of our pastor is terminally ill, or the announcement by the building inspector that certain repairs and changes must be made within thirty days or the meeting house will be padlocked. The petty divisions that fostered those adversarial relationships fade into insignificance in the face of what is perceived as a genuine crisis.

The problem is no one knows how to create the crisis that unifies people around a common goal and still remain out of jail.

That leads to the third and, for some people the most terrifying alternative. Take the steps necessary to resolve the conflict that feeds the fires of adversarial relationships. Conflict resolution is not the subject of this book, but perhaps it should be the top priority in those parishes that are immobilized by adversarial relationships.

What About That Benevolent Dictator?

In today's world an increasing number of people, especially the clergy, are disturbed by any suggestions that appear to affirm a top-down style of ministerial leadership. Few will argue, however, that the benevolent dictator still exists as one of the most common expressions of congregational life. Is this a problem in itself that deserves urgent attention?

The answer is yes and no. If that benevolent dictator (and in smaller congregations that role may be filled by a lay volunteer or by a small clique of volunteers as well as by the minister) consistently opposes any and all proposals to change the status quo, that tendency to veto may become the top priority. This is not a simple problem to resolve!

The most widespread response by churchgoers to that barrier is a silent vote. They vote with their feet and their pocketbook not to support that style of leadership. The younger ones depart for another church with a more open environment. The older ones usually cut back on both their attendance and their participation. Many display a strong attachment to the status quo, but they are disturbed by the complete resistance to even discussing alternative courses of action. Others have proposed or supported what they perceived to be a modest change, but were offended when it was ignored or vetoed without any serious discussion.

A second, but different, expression of authority by the benevolent dictator also may move this up to the top priority on the current agenda. This surfaces when the change-oriented pastor unilaterally pursues counterproductive strategies and nothing happens. This frustrates that minority which is persuaded change is necessary for the continued effective ministry of that parish. This annoys the majority who are content with the status quo. Both groups finally come together on a shared agenda. The time has arrived when we must have a change in ministerial leadership.

The real victim of this coalition is not the benevolent dictator who is forced to resign or to choose early retirement. The victim who merits sincere sympathy often is the successor. That successor arrives, having been persuaded the issue is the approach to ministerial leadership. The new minister comes with a promise to exercise a far more democratic style of leadership. That is widely assumed to be the number-one issue. It turns out, however, that is only a means-to-an-end issue. The number-one pressing problem is how to agree on a strategy for ministry in today's world when one group of leaders want to do yesterday over again, only better, while a smaller group is convinced substantial changes are long overdue. A failure to adapt to a changing world often is the most highly visible legacy of the inept benevolent dictator—and the successor becomes the victim of that failure.

On the other hand, at least a half dozen different scenarios exist in which the leadership style of that benevolent dictator is not a significant issue on the current agenda. One is the relatively new and very rapidly growing new mission, which reports a net gain of one hundred or more in worship attendance year after year. The people joining these new missions are coming to have their religious needs met. Rarely do they display a lust for power or control. A second is in the large and numerically growing congregation which offers an exceptionally high quality and varied seven-day-a-week ministry.[10] A third is the successor to the inept, non-directive, lazy, or laissez-faire pastor who leaves behind a legacy of frustrated members who are impatient to see something happen. They are eager to accept the tradeoff of dictatorial leadership in favor of progress. A fourth is the highly personable, amazingly energetic, highly productive, and ever smiling minister who can cause most of the volunteer leaders to believe, "I am one of our pastor's three or four closest personal friends." A fifth is the pastor who always produces results that exceed the expectations of nearly every ally. A sixth is the very large congregation averaging more than 4,000 at worship. In these congregations it is unrealistic to expect volunteers to be able to know enough about all facets of congregational life to be able to offer informed judgments.

In general, the benevolent dictator tends to be acceptable in the numerically growing organization in which the results, especially in terms of quality, greatly exceed people's expectations. That style of leadership usually tends to be rejected when (a) the organization is shrinking in size and/or (b) goals are not being achieved. It is compatible with change, but not with decline or efforts to perpetuate yesterday.

More important than the style of leadership, however, is what can be done in the absence of the benevolent dictator or the strong initiating leader? What can be done when the climate for change is not supportive of brilliant new ideas? What can be done if everyone is comfortable with the status quo?

Chapter Three

Who Stirs Up the Discontent?

O ne of the most difficult tasks in this world is to enlist
support for change when everyone is contented with the
status quo.

Five or six decades ago, when the American population con-
tained a large number of farmers and thousands of automobile
salesmen (in recent decades most farmers have been replaced by
farm managers and automobile salesmen have been replaced by
order takers), the salesman would drive a new car called a
"demonstrator" out to show the farmer. Typically, the farmer dis-
played zero interest in purchasing a new car and encouraged the
salesman to depart so the farmer could finish his chores before
dark. "I have a car that satisfies all our needs. I can't afford to
trade it in, and I'm busy. If I had any money to spare, I would
buy a new tractor. Thanks for stopping by, but I'm not in the
market for a new car today."

The effective salesman was not discouraged that easily.
"Here're the keys. Why don't you go in, get the missus, and take
her for a spin. She'll enjoy a ride in a new car, and it won't cost
you a nickel. Do your wife a favor and take her for a ride."

The farmer had absolutely no interest in spending the money
he did not have to trade his old car in for a new one he couldn't
afford, but finally he agreed. After all, it would not cost anything
and that ride could be an interesting little break in the dull rou-

tine of farm work. He persuaded his wife to go along. While they waited for her to change her dress and pretty her face, the salesman explained the features on that shiny new automobile, instructed the farmer on how the transmission worked, and deliberately underestimated how much money would be required for a trade.

After a six or seven mile ride, which included a five-minute stop to get an opinion from a respected neighbor, the demonstration was over. During those twenty minutes, the farmer and his wife convinced themselves this new car did have many unexpected advantages over their seven-year-old clunker.

Fifty years ago, that was described as effective salesmanship. For this chapter, that illustrates the concept of the self-identified discrepancy. The car salesman knew he did not possess the persuasive verbal skills required to talk this farmer into trading cars. Instead he created a situation that caused the farmer and his wife to identify the discrepancies between their old vehicle, which, despite its shortcomings, they had expected to retain for at least a few more years, and this attractive new automobile.

One approach to change, which was described in chapter 1, is for the widely trusted leader to initiate it. The support that is gathered is motivated primarily by the earned respect accorded this trusted minister. A second approach, referred to in chapter 2, is the progressive, respected, and exceptionally competent benevolent dictator who unilaterally decides what needs to be done. When this approach is analyzed, it usually turns out that if it works, it is acceptable because it does work. The performance legitimizes the method.

A third approach, which most leaders will find to be both more comfortable and more effective, consists of two components.

Who Identifies That Discrepancy?

By definition, planned change initiated from within an organization does not happen unless there is discontent with the status quo. Frequently the minister is the first, and sometimes the only one to display any significant discontent with the status quo. That simple fact often tempts the minister to act unilaterally. That may work if the pastor has earned the respect of nearly everyone, as described in chapter 1, or if that minister is an exceptionally competent benevolent dictator, as described in chapter 2.

Those two scenarios do not fit the vast majority of pastors, however, so what is an acceptable alternative?

A third alternative begins with the identification and enlistment of allies. Occasionally the allies are drawn from among those who also are discontented with the status quo. Thus the first responsibility of the pastor is to bring together those who already are discontented. Rarely, however, is this sufficient. If that existing cadre did represent sufficient support for change, it already should have happened.

A Crucial Distinction

The presence of substantial discontent, but the absence of any creative results is not uncommon. The explanation is the huge gap between agreement that the status quo no longer is acceptable and securing sufficient support to turn one particular vision for a new tomorrow into reality. Before examining that step in the process of planned change, however, it is necessary to look more carefully at that combination of allies and the self-identified discrepancy.

Three Alternatives

One alternative is largely informal. This is to enlist individuals to see what could be done or to examine needs. As they do this, many of these potential allies will identify the discrepancy between what could be and contemporary reality.

If the issue is an overcrowded Sunday school room up on the second floor, the trustees are asked to visit the second floor during the Sunday school hour. Since most of them usually are doing something else on the first floor during that hour, this can be an eye-opening experience for many of them.

If the issue is an obsolete and worn-out building, a group of volunteers spend a day visiting another congregation, which five years ago met in a similar building and now enjoys a recently completed new church home. If the goal is to raise more money to help alleviate world hunger, the regional judicatory of that denomination plans a mission trip so members can see the need and contrast it with their own comfortable life-style.

If the issue is to add a second worship service on Sunday morning, a group of volunteers go away to worship with a similar congregation that expanded their schedule two years ago. After participating in both worship services, these visitors stay and talk with the people who had initiated that schedule to discover how they view it now. These volunteers see the discrepancy between what is and what could be.

If the issue is to raise more money to support world missions, a group of leaders spend a week or two visiting several mission stations to see firsthand the discrepancy between needs and resources.

If the proposal calls for adding a three-hour after-school program for children every Wednesday afternoon, one alternative is to talk about all the reasons why this would not work here. A better course of action is to enlist a dozen leaders who will spend two or three hours for three consecutive Wednesdays visiting congregations with this ministry. At the end of the month, these volunteers can identify the discrepancy between nothing and an attractive program.

The second of these alternatives is a more structured effort to help individuals identify the discrepancy between a vision of a new and better tomorrow and contemporary reality. Typically this is described as a long-range planning committee or a futures committee or the year 2000 committee or some similar identification that carries a future orientation.

The typical three-part assignment for this committee consists of (a) agreeing on a vision of what the Lord is calling this congregation to be and to be doing five to ten years hence, (b) defining what will be required to turn that vision into reality, and (c) outlining the steps to be taken to implement that vision.[1]

The third alternative does not focus on individuals, but rather on bringing together the appropriate boards, organizations, committees, and commissions to create a new coalition. Thus if the issue is improved facilities for the Sunday school, the coalition might consist of trustees, the finance committee, and the Christian education committee. If the issue is designing a new Saturday evening worship service to reach young adults, the coalition may include the worship committee, the music committee, the evangelism committee, and the task force on young adult ministries.

Once again the effort begins with identifying the discrepancy between what is and what could be.

The use of a coalition is more common in interchurch ministries, denominational structures, and middlesized-to-large congregations than in small churches or very large parishes.

The common thread running through all three alternatives is to bring together a group of volunteers who will identify the discrepancy between what is and what could be. This not only broadens the base of discontent, it also can be the first step in creating the initiating group needed to create that proposed course of action.

Why Do Coalitions Fail?

At first glance, it might appear the best of these three alternatives would be the coalition of boards, organizations, committees, and commissions. This promises to bring together the current policymakers, access to needed resources, a diversity of viewpoints, and the respected and influential leaders needed to build broad-based support. If the members of these three or four organizations can agree on a course of action, that should almost guarantee success. Why do coalitions fail?

The reasons are many and no one explanation fits all situations, but seven factors surface repeatedly.

The most visible is only when confronted with a serious and

fully recognized crisis do the members of the coalition find it easy to agree on a substantially new and different course of action. To be more precise, the members of the new coalition naturally tend to be advocates for the organization or committee they represent. Turf protection becomes a powerful motivation. The allied coalition brought to a quick end the invasion of Kuwait by Iraq in 1990–91. Within months, nationalism and the protection of turf had replaced the military crisis as the number-one factor motivating the policies of the members of the allied coalition.

Second, since the coalition really is a collection of standing committees, the natural tendency is to function like an expanded standing committee. Thus continuity, tradition, and precedents are extremely influential, just as they are in the negotiations of the typical standing committee.

Third, every time an organization or committee that is a part of the coalition changes leaders, it produces a break in the continuity of the deliberations of the coalition.

Fourth, when new leaders come into office in the component organizations of that coalition, they often place their top priority on the goals, health, and role of their own organization. The goals of the coalition are at best a secondary priority.

Fifth, most of the meaningful psychic rewards for these leaders come out of their work in their own organization, not out of their contributions to the work of the coalition.

Sixth, frequently when a coalition is remarkably effective, the temptation is to believe that success is a product of cooperation. In fact, that success often is largely a product of the choice of a unifying issue. A highly visible example of this was the contributions of the interfaith coalitions on civil rights back in the 1960s. Many hailed that as the beginning of a new era in Protestant, Roman Catholic, Orthodox, and Jewish cooperation. Then came the issues of abortion and homosexuality.

Not infrequently a new issue emerges that either divides the existing coalition or makes it obsolete. In 1939–41 a coalition of forces scattered all along the political spectrum was able to keep the United States out of the war in Europe. Then came Pearl Harbor.

Finally, coalitions are far more likely than ad hoc, long-range planning committees to agree on a watered-down compromise that does not threaten the status quo within any of the participating organizations. By contrast, the ad hoc, long-range planning committee tends to operate on the assumption that everything is permitted and nothing is prohibited. Coalitions are tempted, in order to maintain harmony, to focus first on what is off limits for this group. That limits the creativity of coalitions.

As you seek to initiate change in your congregation, denomination, movement, or parachurch organization, who will identify the discrepancy between what could be and what is? That is a critical early decision in a strategy for planning change.

Once the discrepancy between what is and what could be is lifted up, someone is likely to challenge the authority of those who are preparing a strategy for change.

Chapter Four

Who Gave You the Authority?

T he most frustrating five years of my ministry were spent with what had been organized as a neighborhood church back in 1921," reflected the fifty-two-year-old pastor currently serving a downtown church in a county seat with 6,200 residents and a trading area that included nearly 15,000. "By the time I arrived in 1982, fewer than a dozen families lived within three miles of the church. The population of the central city had increased from 40,000 in 1920 to nearly 200,000 in 1970 when it began to decline. During the 1960s and 1970s most of the folks who could afford to had moved out to the suburbs. The membership of that congregation had dropped from nearly 400 at the peak in 1955 to fewer than 200 when I came, and a good many of them were shut-ins or in nursing homes. They had a well-maintained building with an excellent educational wing that had been completed in 1958. I suggested we carve out a non-geographical niche with a seven-day-a-week ministry with families that had preschool children."

"What happened?" inquired the friend who was listening intently over their mid-morning cup of coffee.

"Nothing," replied the pastor. "They wanted a chaplain, and I wanted to be an evangelist. I simply couldn't enlist any support for what I wanted to do. No one opposed me, they simply refused to do anything. After three years, I began to look for another call, and that's how I ended up here in this place."

"Who was your predecessor back there?" asked the friend.

"I followed a man who had retired after a dozen years," came the reply. "He was greatly loved by everyone, especially by the little old ladies, but about all he did was preach and call. People claimed he called in every home at least six or eight times a year, and I know he called on every shut-in at least once a month. When he retired, that little congregation gave him a farewell gift of $30,000 as a down payment on a retirement home in Florida! And that was in 1983 dollars. That would be the equivalent of close to $50,000 today. I also should add that the membership dropped by about seventy-five during his pastorate, and worship attendance dropped by at least a fourth, but no one ever mentioned that to me while I was there."

"Sounds to me as if he was the full-time resident chaplain they wanted you to be," commented the friend.

"You got it," agreed this pastor. "He was an effective, hard-working, and beloved chaplain."

"Chaplains rarely possess the authority required to initiate and implement radical systemic changes," observed the friend.

*   *   *

"When my wife and I arrived here back in 1977 to plant a new church, the only person we knew was the missions director of the conference," reminisced the senior pastor of a congregation now averaging nearly 1500 in worship every weekend. "I spent the first eight months calling on everybody I could find at home, going to all of the high school ball games open to the public, and dropping in on every shopkeeper, store manager, and professional office. My basic methodology was to plug into existing networks of people who weren't going to church anywhere. As you probably know, chuchgoers tend to socialize with other churchgoers, while the unchurched socialize with other unchurched people. My goal was to relate to the networks among the unchurched. While I was doing that, I worked out the design for this new mission. One of my goals was that we would have at least five hundred people at our first service. We actually had well over six hundred, and the smallest crowd we've ever had was about three hundred. I found this twenty-six acre site, persuaded the owner to sell it to us on a land contract, and today we have $3,000,000 worth of buildings with no debt, and we're getting ready to construct our next unit which will cost us about $4,000,000. My new goal is to exceed two thousand in worship within three more years."

"Who gave you the authority to make all those decisions?" inquired the highly impressed visitor.

"God gave me the authority in my call to come out here and organize this congregation," was the confident reply.

The moral of these two examples taken from real life could be that it may be easier to be a mission developer pastor than to follow the popular chaplain of a passive parish.

A more significant point, however, is that it is difficult to initiate planned change from within an organization without the necessary authority. That raises a fundamental, but widely neglected issue. What are the sources of authority?

For thousands of years rulers have been asked, What is the basis of your authority? The Pharaohs and hundreds of kings answered that they ruled in the name of God. The American and Canadian experiences are based on the assumption that government rules with the consent of the governed, which is tested by periodic elections.

Legend has it that when staff members challenged the late Henry Ford II about a particular decision, Mr. Ford occasionally would explain, "We'll do it that way because it's my name that's on the building."

This question received tremendous coverage in the popular press following the fall of the Berlin Wall, the dissolution of the Soviet Union of Socialist Republics, and the breakup of the nation once known as Yugoslavia.

One answer, of course, is armed power. The burglar armed with a loaded revolver possesses tremendous coercive power over the resident. Likewise a military dictatorship can exercise nearly total control over the lives and actions of the citizens of that nation. This raises a basic distinction that cannot be ignored.

Authority or Power?

Students of this subject often point out that authority is a product of a title or role or office that has legitimacy in the eyes of those who are subjected to that authority. By contrast, power can be acquired through other means. Thus the person who invades your home may not have a legitimate right or authority to order you around, but that loaded gun gives the invader great power over you.

A parallel to that is a minister may serve in a church in which the polity and denominational traditions grant great authority to the pastor, but because of local variables, including the personality of that minister, most of the real power is exercised by volunteer leaders. In other churches a pastor may have earned the respect of the parishioners and thus be able to exercise far more power than is suggested by the words in that congregation's constitution that define the authority of the pastor, the governing board, and other components of the organizational structure.

Another way of contrasting the two is that in a totalitarian society all legitimate authority may be vested in those who monopolize the power. By contrast, in a democratic society authority is granted by the people to those officials who are selected by and accountable to the people.

This question about the basis for the authority of leaders in the churches has come up repeatedly in the history of the Christian churches. One answer has been apostolic succession. Another has been by vote of the people. A third has been by vote of the representatives of the parishioners. A fourth has been by vote of the clergy. A fifth has been seniority and tenure. A sixth has been "God's will." A seventh has been tradition. An eighth has been "I organized this church." A ninth has been bloodlines, and a tenth has been "by default."

Most of the schisms in the Christian churches have followed a challenge to the authority of ecclesiastical leaders. Martin Luther and Roger Williams are but two names in a long list of those who have challenged the traditional sources of authority in the churches. Similar challenges are heard today in many parts of the Christian churches. This continues to rank among the most divisive issues in both congregational and denominational circles.

The North American Spectrum

One frame of reference for reviewing the basis for authority on this continent is to think in terms of a spectrum. At one end of that spectrum are located the Roman Catholic Church, The United Methodist Church, and the Anglican and Episcopal churches. All four place an exceptionally high degree of authority in the office of the bishop and in the office of parish pastor. All four stand out from most of the rest of the Protestant churches on this continent by the authority granted the bishop and the pastor by tradition and polity.

At the other end of this spectrum are those lay-led and lay-controlled congregations that do not have set-apart paid clergy. They differ in several repects, but most of them grant tremendous authority to a handful of individual leaders. This may be on the basis of bloodlines or spiritual gifts or the drawing of lots or age or personality or religious commitment or gender or skill or communication skills or native intelligence or wisdom or wealth or social status or other criteria.

Near that end of the spectrum are those churches that place great authority in the volunteer lay elders and deacons and turn to the Bible (Titus 1:5-6 and Timothy 3:8-13) as the sole authority for the criteria to qualify one to become an elder or a deacon. In some of these churches the pastor is identified as a "teaching minister" or "teaching elder," and that office is not perceived as carrying great authority in matters of policy formulation.

The majority of Christian congregations on the North American continent, however, are scattered along the spectrum between those two extremes. Most of them share one common characteristic. The authority granted leaders by the constitution or polity or tradition or book of church order is shrinking in influence. Likewise neither ordination nor academic degrees carry the authority they once bestowed on the clergy. By contrast, personality, competence, integrity, good judgment, commitment, and vision continue to be crucial sources of authority in both congregational and denominational circles. Paper credentials, such as diplomas, degrees, and ordination certificates, no longer carry the weight they once did. While they are not as influential as they once were, friendship ties, wealth, gender, bloodlines, age, and tenure continue as important sources of authority in the churches.

From Given to Earned

The big change in recent decades in American Protestantism, however, is the shift from bestowed to earned authority. Once upon a time, a parish pastor acquired a significant degree of authority by ordination and/or by being called or installed as the pastor. The title and office carried considerable weight. This was more obvious in Lutheran parishes than in Baptist congregations, but to varying degrees it was true all across that spectrum of churches described earlier. A parallel trend is the challenging, or even more interesting, the ignoring of the authority of bishops in Catholic, Methodist, and Anglican traditions.

Today few pastors can depend on ordination, title, and office as sources of authority. Today authority must be earned. Today it is not unusual for many of the volunteers to have more earned academic degrees than have been granted the pastor. A few may have greater mastery of the law of the church than is possessed by the pastor. Others may know more than the pastor does about church finances or real estate or pedagogical skills or group dynamics or planning or counseling or theology.

The pastors who are the respected and influential leaders in their congregations today have earned their authority. It is not simply the product of theological training or ordination or a title or an office. The authority for their leadership has been earned by vision, competence, performance, skill, character, knowledge, creativity, hard work, wisdom, productivity, initiative, and verbal skills.

Nations and Denominations

Another useful contemporary perspective for reflecting on authority are the pressures on the nation state. The breakup in Pakistan in 1971, the separatist movements in the Middle East, the collapse of the Soviet Union, and the disintegration of Yugoslavia are recent and current examples of the challenges to the legitimacy and power of the nation state.

Professor Stephen Philip Cohen of the University of Illinois at Urbana-Champaign recently identified five factors that have undercut the authority of the state.

1. Modern technologies have weakened the ability of nations to control information. Jet aircraft, FAX machines, cassette recorders, VCRs, small transistor radios, and satellite broadcasting systems have democratized the flow of information across national boundaries.

2. Nations no longer can protect their citizens in wartime. Iraq stands out as the number-one example in the early 1990s. National defense no longer is a unifying role for a nation.

3. Nations no longer can guarantee economic prosperity. The states that once constituted the Soviet Union are but one of many examples.

4. Once upon a time it was assumed that the object of politics is justice, and nations were expected to perpetuate justice. Today a huge variety of self appointed agencies ranging from Amnesty International to the World Bank to the United Nations see themselves as the guarantors of justice.

5. Separatist groups can work from within to undermine the national unity the nation once guaranteed. Contemporary examples include Canada, Pakistan, Yugoslavia, India, Iraq, China, and Russia.

Add to that list the traditional functions of government such as protection of persons and property, creation and maintenance of transportation networks, promotion of the health and welfare of the citizens, and control over the borders, and it is easy to see why scholars are questioning the future of the nation state.

In simple language the traditional foundations for the authority of the nation are being undermined.

The parallel has been occurring within denominational structures.

What have been the traditional sources of authority for denominations? While it would be difficult to secure wide support for the content and ranking of any list, these twelve would be a part of most explanations for the authority vested in denominations.

1. Design and perpetuate orthodoxy and oppose heresy.

2. Design and authorize the proper forms of worship and the proper administration of the sacraments.

3. Examine and credential the clergy.

4. Organize, staff, and mobilize support for world missions.

5. Publish hymnals and worship aids and provide other resources for congregations.

6. Organize new congregations.

7. Create and perpetuate a sense of unity within that movement or tradition.

8. Provide theological seminaries for the preparation of the next generation of clergy.

9. Serve as the liaison with and critic of government as part of a larger prophetic witness.

10. Create new nonparochial ministries including homes, hospitals, colleges, and so on.

11. Serve as the basic structure for interdenominational and interfaith conversations and cooperation.

12. For a few, to control the placement of the clergy as parish pastors.

Today denominational leaders are more likely to be accused of heresy than of ferreting it out; congregational leaders design their own worship services; credentials carry less weight; scores of parachurch organizations recruit, place, and support missionaries; parachurch agencies, megachurches, and entrepreneurial individuals are publishing hymnals and offering many other resources for congregations; megachurches, seminary professors, Bible school graduates, and entrepreneurial ministers are planting at least half of all new congregations; denominational unity has been severely eroded, but few seem to care; transdenominational seminaries are growing at the expense of the denominational seminaries; televangelists, megachurch pastors, coalitions of congregations, and parachurch organizations are serving as critics of government; the historic nonparochial, denominationally created institutions are renouncing denominational control; coalitions of pastors and/or congregations have become the building blocks for the new interchurch coalitions and lay leaders want to choose their own pastor.

Many of the traditional sources of authority have been eroded by the forces of change. That is one reason that denominations are being written off as "cultural dinosaurs" or "irrelevant self-appointed regulatory agencies." More significant, however, is that erosion of authority makes it difficult to create the alliance required for reform. "Who gave you the authority to initiate reform in my denomination?" Thus when some reformers find their authority under challenge, they simply depart and create a new religious movement. (See chapter 7.)

The Big Illusion

Perhaps the greatest—and riskiest—temptation for the self-identified initiator of planned change is to assume that a brilliant idea or a carefully thought out plan automatically carries considerable authority simply on its own merits. One of the most common examples of this is the individual or the ad hoc citizens' committee who appears at the public hearing scheduled by a department of a state or local government. Frequently these dedicated, concerned—and naive—volunteers come to submit what they are persuaded is a more meritorious proposal. The issue may be the center line for a new freeway or a change in zoning or the proposed municipal budget for the coming year or a change in the boundaries of an elementary school district. These concerned citizens come expecting that merit will be the decisive factor in the decision-making process. They are disappointed and often disillusioned when they discover that the voice of authority is more influential than the merits of their proposal.

Similar incidents occur repeatedly at the annual meetings of congregations, regional judicatories, and national denominational gatherings such as general assemblies, general conferences, and general synods.

The First Lesson

Back in 1892 Victor Hugo wrote, "An invasion of armies can be resisted, but not an idea whose time has come."

That memorable statement oversimplifies life. A more realistic statement would include the caveat that there must be a broad-based acceptance of the belief that the time for change has arrived. Thus the first lesson in this discussion on the place of authority in planned change is simple. Do not assume merit will be an effective substitute for authority.

Two More Lessons

A related lesson for the initiator of planned change is that authority usually rests in institutions and individuals, not in ideas alone, no matter how brilliant that idea may be in the eyes of those who conceived it. Every proposal for change, regardless of how brilliant it may be, requires a support group for implementation.

The third lesson is that while the rules may grant one vote to every person, some votes are more influential than others. When the president of the United States meets with the cabinet, the president's vote usually constitutes a majority. Likewise, the larger the size of the congregation and/or the more rapid the rate of numerical growth, the more likely the vote of the senior minister will carry more weight than the vote of any six other individuals, including staff.

At the other end of that spectrum are the long-established small congregations in which bloodlines and friendship ties are the two most powerful cohesive forces. In these churches the opposition of one influential veteran member may more than offset the support of a half dozen newcomers.

In a democratic society authority is rarely dispensed in uniform amounts to every citizen. How is it dispensed? Among the Christian churches in North America, the answer is from among a variety of sources.

A Fourth Lesson

One of the most widely ignored lessons from experience is illustrated by the opening case study in this chapter. A leader needs far less authority when the goal is to perpetuate the status quo than is needed when the goal is planned change to be initiated from within that organization. Thus the minister who spent a dozen years as the resident chaplain needed far less authority for that role than was required by that impatient short-tenured successor who wished to redefine the role of that parish.

A Fifth Lesson

Finally, before moving on to a review of the most common sources of authority, a word of caution should be raised. One facet of this lesson is the importance of redundancy. Do not place all your eggs in one basket. It is wiser to affirm the value of benefiting from several sources of authority. The other side of this coin is that some people will accept one or two sources of authority while rejecting all other sources. Therefore, the wise agent of planned change will actively seek the legitimacy of several sources of authority. What will not be an acceptable source for many will be fully acceptable for others.

Eight Sources

"In the land of the blind, the one-eyed man is king," declares an ancient adage. The contemporary translation is that knowledge is the greatest single source of power in our world today. One of the most effective ways to undermine the authority that goes with the office of pastor is to reply to questions asked by parishioners with such answers as, "I really don't know," or "I have no idea of how we should deal with that," or "Don't ask me."

Forgetting for the moment the textbook distinction between power and authority, one of the ways pastors earn the role of a respected leader is by being prepared to offer informed, credible, and relevant responses to questions parishioners raise about the life, ministry, and resources of that congregation.

The person who knows far more about a particular subject than anyone else in the room and who is able to apply that knowledge in a meaningful way to that discussion, usually will enjoy an influential voice.

Three cautions should be added lest knowledge be overrated as a source of authority. The most obvious is in groups that are organized around interpersonal relationships. In these groups, relational skills usually are far more influential sources of authority than is knowledge. A common example is the highly educated and newly arrived pastor who comes to that first meeting of the governing board of that hundred-year-old small working class congregation. The new pastor's carefully thought-out and expertly prepared mission statement is given a cordial reception, but nothing changes. The top priority for these veteran volunteer leaders is, "Does our new minister love us?" That mission statement is irrelevant to that agenda. One way to demonstrate one's love is to listen intently, respectfully, and responsively to the needs articulated by the people. Another is to be present in time of need.

A second exception is when the bearer of knowledge is an outsider who has not yet won the trust and confidence of the insiders. This exceptionally knowledgeable agent of change may be a new member or the pastor or a staff person from denominational headquarters or an outside third party consultant with no institutional ties to that congregation. The top priority for that knowledgeable individual is not to share that wealth of wisdom. The first priority is to win the trust and confidence of the insiders. This helps to explain why the advice of the outside expert who comes in for a two-hour meeting on Tuesday evening often is ignored. The content of the advice may have matched the needs perfectly, but it did not carry any authority.

A third exception is when radical change is the real issue. In these circumstances the power of the status quo may offset the weight of knowledge. Common illustrations of this include the meeting called to slash the proposed budget of a regional judicatory, the family that has come together to persuade the seventy-four-year-old grandmother to move out of the house she has lived in for forty years to enter a nursing home, the proposal to relocate the meeting place of the hundred-year-old congregation, or the unexpected recommendation of the doctor for major surgery. Knowledge does not always carry the day.

A second source of authority that no longer is as influential as it once was has been referred to earlier. This is the authority that is automatically vested in the person who holds a particular office. The titles vary, but it often is assumed that title or office does confer authority on the holder. President, manager, foreman, department head, mayor, professor, bishop, governor, mother, secretary, superintendent, principal, pastor, father, doctor, coach, husband, judge, senator, director, and general are examples of titles that once carried substantial authority. Some still do, but not in all circumstances.

From an ecclesiastical perspective this source often is described as polity. In governmental circles it usually begins with a constitution. As was pointed out earlier, one end of the polity spectrum in North America grants huge quantities of authority to individuals such as bishops and pastors while at the other end of that spectrum nearly all authority is vested in the congregation.

A third source has many facets and often is overlooked. This is what sociologists describe as the deference pyramid and most people refer to as "the pecking order." This continues to be a visible source of authority in nearly every organization. In North America eight of the most common factors in the deference pyramid have been (1) age—younger people have been expected to defer to older people, (2) seniority—newcomers are expected to defer to long-tenured people, (3) salary—people paid a lower salary are expected to defer to those paid a higher salary, (4) formal education—those with less formal education have been expected to defer to those with more formal education (perhaps the number-one contemporary example is reflected in the expectations physicians project toward nurses), (5) gender—women have been expected to defer to men, (6) title—people with less impressive titles have been expeted to defer to those with more impressive titles, (7) ordination—lay people have been expected to defer to ordained ministers, and (8) ancestry and/or nationality heritage—people who do not share the status-conferring bloodlines are expected to defer to those who do possess that advantage.

The reason some of these are referred to in the past tense is that the wave of egalitarianism that swept across North America in the second half of the twentieth century has undermined at least three or four of the assumptions on which the deference pyramid rests.[1]

The deference pyramid still is a significant source of authority in many big congregations, in most large corporations, in the Catholic, Anglican, and Methodist religious traditions, to a gradually decreasing degree in Lutheran circles, in the theologically very conservative churches, in most multiple staff relationships, in the majority of large black congregations, in many long-established small churches, and in most Asian churches.

A fourth source of authority that is increasingly influential can be summarized in four words—hard and productive work. This does not necessarily mean long hours. It does mean hard work and making productive use of that time. That also is a source of knowledge.

Overlapping a couple of these sources is the one that many believe should rank at the top of the list. This is competence. The obvious caveat on this is that the competence of the leader must match the needs of that organization. One example is the highly introverted minister who is an exceptionally competent scholar, but because of a shortage of research positions ends up as a parish pastor. The need in that parish may be for an extroverted, moral, loving, gentle, and gregarious personality, not for competence as a scholar. Competence is a source of authority only when that competence matches the need. When competence produces a high level of performance, that can be a powerful source of authority! Competence and performance stand out as especially significant sources of authority in the small democratic institutions that function as voluntary associations. Competence is less significant as a source of authority in hierarchical institutions. Thus a regional minister in the Christian Church (Disciples of Christ) or a conference minister in the United Church of Christ or a director of missions in a Southern Baptist Association is far more likely to see their authority being evaluated on the basis of competence and performance than will a bishop in the Roman Catholic Church or The United Methodist Church. The relatively incompetent bishop can survive by depending on office, tradition, personality, polity, and title as sources of authority. The regional minister in The United Church of Christ who possesses an identical level of competence will experience great difficulties.

One of the broadest sources of authority is what one scholar identifies as personal choice.[2] A common example of this is the founding pastor of a new congregation who continues in that position for decades. At the end of twenty years that minister can explain, "When they joined this congregation, every one of our present members knew that I would be their pastor. When they picked this church, they knew I would be their pastor."

When combined with twenty years of seniority, competent performance, knowledge, title, the deference pyramid, and hard work, that explains why the senior minister of the church that now averages over a thousand at worship is often perceived to be a benevolent dictator.

At the other extreme of that spectrum is the newly arrived United Methodist pastor who was appointed by the bishop following a perfunctory meeting by the district superintendent and the pastor parish relations committee. That new minister is not the personal choice of any member and must earn acceptance and trust.

Between those points on this spectrum is the recently arrived senior minister who was called to succeed the founding pastor after a twenty-year tenure. The search committee interviewed a dozen candidates, narrowed the list to three, interviewed each of those three a second time, and finally chose one minister as their unanimous choice. That candidate arrived and spent three days studying the community, meeting with each staff member, with other volunteer leaders, and with several committees, perhaps preached one Sunday morning, and subsequently received a unanimous vote at a heavily attended meeting to be called as the next senior minister. For that new senior minister, the factor of personal choice can be the source of considerable authority.

By contrast, the new senior minister of the United Methodist church down the street may have to depend on other sources for the authority required to be an effective leader.

Under this broad umbrella of personal choice also are placed such factors as earned trust, skill, experience, personality, friendship ties, charisma, character, tenure, verbal skills, and confidence.

A seventh source of authority sometimes is described simply as economy.[3] The most obvious example is those churches with a congregational polity that elect several members to serve as a governing board. They also delegate a degree of authority to various standing committees. Instead of scheduling forty or fifty meetings of the entire congregation every year, for reasons of economy of time and energy, they delegate authority to a church council and several committees. The final authority does rest with the entire congregation. Instead of calling a new preacher every week, they call a minister for a term of three years or, perhaps, for an open-ended period of time. If and when that call is for life, that represents a near-permanent assignment of authority to the minister.

Likewise it is not uncommon for that congregation to assign a responsibility to an ad hoc committee or task force with the authority to make a final and irrevocable decision on that one specific issue.

Whenever a voluntary association staffed entirely by volunteers reaches the point where they decide to hire paid staff, this factor of economy emerges as a source of authority. "I don't have the time for more meetings, let the director (secretary, pastor, nurse, denominational staff person, et al.) decide what to do."

Another common expression of economy as a source of authority is reflected in the decision to call the young and popular associate minister as the successor to the senior pastor who is retiring after twenty years. "Why spend all that time, energy, and money looking at unknowns when we have a known and tested minister right here on our staff?"

Finally, the last, and perhaps the most subjective of these eight sources of authority is the widely perceived crisis. The key words in that sentence are *widely perceived.* It would be easy to fill a thick book with examples of congregations, regional judicatories, denominational agencies, interchurch organizations, and theological seminaries that experienced great difficulties because no one responded to a crisis until too late. Back when the problem was still perceived to be a minor irritation that time would cure, no one possessed the authority or the initiative required for preventive action. Gradually the passage of time eliminated one potentially productive course of action after another from the list of alternatives.

Eventually the list of alternatives was reduced to two—unattractive choice A and unattractive choice B. Finally, nearly everyone agrees we are confronted with a severe crisis. Who will be granted the authority to resolve the crisis?

At this point title, polity, the deference pyramid, and perhaps even personal choice disappear from the list as sources of authority. Competence (or at least perceived competence), economy, and perhaps knowledge float to the top of the list of criteria. The critical one, however, is the willingness to take on what appears to be an impossible challenge.

This helps to explain why the church-related college with a dwindling enrollment that has been using reserves to balance the budget suddenly is open to calling as the new president a person who does not come from that religious tradition and has never worked in an academic institution. That candidate, however, is perceived as possessing the skills required to resolve the crisis and is granted far more authority than ever accorded a fully credentialed predecessor.

The widely perceived crisis changes the rules. That also explains why some agents of change begin by attempting to persuade everyone this institution is confronted with a crisis. If successful, that can become a source of authority.

The Parish Context

While most of the sources discussed here can be found in nearly every institution in our society ranging from governments to hospitals to profitmaking corporations to amateur sports teams to service clubs, the assignment of authority by congregations does have a few special nuances that merit a brief word. In more specific terms, these ten variables usually have to be assessed in determining the authority and power of the pastor in that situation.

One is the size of the congregation. As a general rule, the larger the size of the congregation, the greater the influence of the pastor or senior minister in formulating policy and making decisions.

A second is tenure. The longer the tenure of the pastor, the more likely the passage of time has increased the influence of the pastor.

A third is seniority. As was pointed out earlier, the founding pastor of a new mission normally has far greater power and influence than a subsequent successor who arrives to find every member has seniority over the new minister. No successor can benefit to the same degree from personal choice. Every successor inherits members who did not join because of personal choice of preferring that pastor.

A fourth is the combination of age and experience. Patients often grant greater control over their lives to the forty-year-old physician who has performed a particular surgical procedure seven hundred times than they will to the thirty-year-old who has always wanted to perform that operation, but never before had the chance.

A fifth, which can be extremely influential, is polity. As was pointed out earlier, some denominations and congregations vest great authority in the office of pastor. Others place most of the authority in volunteer leaders or in the members.

A sixth is that combination of four factors described earlier (knowledge, hard and productive work, trustworthiness, and offering advice that can stand the test of time). Together these may be more significant than polity, tenure, seniority, and size.

A seventh overlaps the sixth, but deserves special recognition. This is an exceptionally high level of performance. In some congregations that exceptionally competent church secretary or that remarkably able and loyal volunteer treasurer have earned a veto over almost any proposal for change. Performance can be a powerful source of authority, especially among volunteers.

An eighth factor that frequently is overlooked was illustrated in the opening paragraphs of this chapter. That is the predecessor. If the predecessor did not claim much authority, no one expects the successor to hold much authority. If the predecessor earned the respect, trust, and confidence of almost every parishioner and thus was granted great authority as a leader, the successor may find it easy to move into the role of an influential leader in that congregation if he or she is able and willing to do so. Likewise, if widespread distrust of the predecessor's competence, integrity, leadership, character, or religous commitment led to the departure of that predecessor, it usually will be neccessary for the successor to restore the people's confidence and respect for the office of pastor before assuming an influential leadership role.

The ninth can be seen most clearly (a) among some of the staff members of very large churches and (b) among several of the volunteer workers in the smaller churches. This factor is character. It can outweigh knowledge, competence, performance, skill, the deference pyramid, hard work, economy, or other factors in the delegation of authority. An interesting example is the small, working-class church served by a male pastor with a modest level of competence. He possesses few other valuable qualifications, but is married to a wife who is almost universally perceived to be a saintly person. Her character can win considerable authority for her husband.

The last variable, which many will argue should be at the top of this list, is that combination of personality, leadership skills, spiritual gifts, and vision. While these are all subjective factors, they are most conspicuous by their absence. The pastor who scores very high on all four of these characteristics usually is granted authority as a leader far beyond what is called for by polity, seniority, tenure, size of parish, age, experience, and other variables.

One Discordant Note

While it surfaces only rarely, one other source of authority exists in some parishes organized around a congregational polity. This is membership. Occasionally this emerges as an unexpected source of authority to veto a proposed change.

One memorable illustration is the three-hundred-member congregation that had always been served by male pastors. When the current pastor retired after seventeen pleasant, but uneventful years, the fifteen-member search committee interviewed a dozen candidates and finally recommended a forty-seven-year-old divorced mother. She was the overwhelming favorite of the search committee and received a unanimous vote. The twenty-four member governing board received that recommendation and, after interviewing the candidate, unanimously recommended her to the congregation.

A dozen active members objected to her candidacy, a few because they disapproved of the ordination of women, others because she was a divorced single parent. Together they persuaded nearly a hundred resident members, most of them relatively inactive, plus a score of non-resident members, to attend the congregational meeting and vote against the recommended call. The final vote was 143 in favor of calling her and 126 in opposition. Given that modest majority, the candidate was advised to refuse the call. She did, and five months later the congregation called a fifty-one-year-old divorced male pastor.

Was that a fair decision? The answer is, Yes! if you believe membership should be the number-one source of authority.

Questions

1. What are the most important sources of authority in your congregation?
2. How many of these are dependent on the gifts of the minister and which ones are the product of your polity or system of governance?

3. Does your present pastor have more or less authority and power than that held by the predecessor? Why?

4. Who are the chief rivals to your pastor for authority? Why? Is that changing?

The answers to these questions on authority may help you decide who has the right to initiate change.

Chapter Five

Who Decides?

"If you ask me, I believe we need the support of the vast majority of our members before we undertake any major changes here," urged the sixty-seven-year-old Harold Lindstrom to the recently arrived pastor at the three-hundred-member Grace Church. "I know we're going to have to make some changes around here in the next few years. Our members are getting older and our attendance is down from what it was only a few years ago. We do have to attract a new generation if we're going to survive, but I believe everybody understands that. Our last pastor was not in the best of health for several years. When his wife died two years ago, that took all the starch out of him. It was apparent to everybody that he was ready to retire long before he did. Now we need to make some changes, and I believe everyone understands that. You're young, we know you're a good preacher, and we have great hopes for what you can do for this church, but don't go too fast. Be sure to get the people behind you before you propose any radical changes."

What do you think of that advice?

A two-day visit to that congregation by a parish consultant revealed several bits of relevant data, (1) the new minister is a gifted, energetic, creative, personable, experienced, visionary, enthusiastic, and impatient thirty-five year old who has aroused expectations that a flood of young couples will be attracted by this new pastor's preaching, personality, and charm; (2) the real estate needs a minimum of $350,000 in improvements to meet contemporary standards including offstreet parking, meeting rooms, and the mechanical systems; (3) at least three dozen parents in their forties hope the new pastor will re-create the type of youth program they enjoyed when they were teenagers; (4) the beloved sixty-three-year-old, part-time organist-choir director hates anything resembling modern religious music and is convinced the term *contemporary Christian music* is an oxymoron; (5) the one adult Sunday school class consists of fifteen people, nine of whom are past sixty; (6) over the past seven years an average of 10 percent of total expenditures have been allocated for missions; (7) during the past seven years a total of twenty adults have joined this parish by letter of transfer—and eight of these were "retreads," former members who had moved away and returned; (8) during the past seven years the average attendance at worship had dropped from 155 to 123; (9) a check of the membership roster revealed names and addresses were available for only 217 of those reported three hundred members; (10) total receipts from member contributions had been on a plateau for the past five years; (11) the average attendance in the Sunday school was down to 47; (12) the second youngest person on the nine-member governing board is fifty-four; (13) nearly everyone interviewed expressed a wish that the new pastor would re-create the kind of congregation they remembered this to be fifteen years earlier; and (14) only three members openly regretted the retirement and departure of the former pastor.

It could be argued a far-above average openness to change exists in this eighty-eight year-old congregation. That, however, is far from broad-based support for a specific long-range strategy.

What happened?

Nine years later this congregation was reporting an average attendance of eighty-five at the seven o'clock Saturday evening worship experience, one hundred at the eight-thirty Sunday morning service, and well over two hundred at the eleven o'clock service. The eighty-year-old parsonage on the east side of the building had been razed and replaced by a two-story educational and office wing. The three-story Sunday school building on the west side, constructed in 1927, was razed. The five remaining houses on the west side had been purchased and demolished. That entire area was now a 135-space parking lot. The old red brick church building had been completely renovated at a cost of over $400,000. During these nine years a total of nearly five hundred adults had united with Grace Church—about three hundred by letter of transfer, the rest by reaffirmation of faith or profession of faith or adult baptism. One-half of this second group were adults who had been reared in the Roman Catholic Church. Twenty percent of the operating budget is now allocated for missions. A total of 138 of those 217 members who had welcomed this new pastor nine years earlier were still active members. All but a half dozen were enthusiastic supporters of the new reality—about a dozen of those 217 had left to join another congregation in town because of their dissatisfaction with the changes. Three or four others had simply dropped out and their names had been removed from the membership roster. The others either had moved away or died.

How Did It Happen?

How had that energetic and visionary pastor been able to mobilize broad-based support for all these changes? This was that pastor's response to the question.

"I didn't. Only a half dozen of our members were active supporters of the Saturday evening service. All but two members of our board either opposed it or were neutral. I put together a planning committee of thirty-five young adults, three of whom were members here, to design that service. We targeted the eighteen-to-twenty-two-year-old population. Two of those five had fathers on our board. That is why they supported me."

"Didn't you need a vote of approval to go ahead with that?" interrupted one of the people to whom this pastor was explaining what had happened.

"No and yes," replied the pastor. "No, I did not ask my board or our members for approval. All I needed was the withholding of a veto. Yes, we did need approval of that eighteen-to-twenty-two-year-old crowd. They voted first by serving on the planning committee and later by inviting their friends. At the time, no other church in this area offered a worship service for young adults. I didn't know whether it would work or not. The only way we could determine that was by trying it. The only meaningful vote rested with those young adults."

"How about razing the parsonage?" asked someone else. "Didn't that require a congregational vote?"

"Yes, it did," agreed this pastor, "but that wasn't the key decision. The crucial decision was when the trustees decided they did not want to spend a lot of money on renovating that dilapidated, old, frame Sunday school wing or renovating that run-down parsonage. About six of us made the three critical decisions. The first was to raze the Sunday school wing and turn that space into parking. The second was the only obvious related step, which was to replace it before we tore it down. The third was to raze the parsonage rather than remodel it. Once those three decisions had been made and implemented, that meant we planned to stay here rather than relocate. That also meant we needed to control this side of the block, so when the first of those remaining five houses came on the market, we bought it. After that, it was just taken for granted we would buy the other four whenever an owner decided to sell."

"I can't believe it was that easy," exclaimed someone else in the group of nine to whom this story was being told.

"It wasn't," replied the pastor. "Soon after I arrived, I realized my biggest battle would be over music. That thirty-five-person planning committee I mentioned earlier decided on the music for Saturday night. Our part-time organist-choir director was offended when she discovered she had not even been consulted, but that came after the first Saturday evening service. Likewise, I put together a planning committee of fifteen to design the early Sunday morning service. No one in that group even considered asking her advice and she was offended by that. By that time, she was sixty-seven. When she came into my office one morning to announce she was resigning, I knew I was in trouble if I accepted it. She has at least a dozen close friends here who would have created a storm if they thought I had forced her out."

"What did you do?" interrupted someone.

"I told her I did not have the authority to accept her letter of resignation. All I could do was receive it and refer it to the board. She took that as a victory and left happy. I took her letter to the board, asked them to create a three-person ad hoc committee with the authority to respond to it. That was done. The ad hoc committee took her letter literally and negotiated with her the date of her last day on the payroll and a terminal leave payment, and planned a big farewell dinner to honor her. I wasn't involved in that meeting, but as I understand it, the only decision they left to her was the date of the party. I was the master of the ceremonies. After it was over, her friends came up to thank me for all the wonderful things I did and said. A couple of them denounced the ad hoc committee for not persuading her to withdraw her letter of resignation, but they were pleased with the recognition and affirmation she received that night."

"I have a question," said one of the group. "Was there ever one time when the congregation or your board looked at this whole package and voted yea or nay on the entire batch of changes?"

"Nope, I believe in incremental change," was the reply.

"One last question," called out someone else. "What was the largest number of people ever involved in making any one of the decisions in this whole sequence of changes?"

"That's impossible to answer," replied the pastor, "but let me give you a few examples. As I told you earlier we had thirty-five people make the key decisions on the Saturday evening service, we had fifteen make the decisions on the new early service. We have seven trustees, and together we originated all the recommendations on real estate. That three-person ad hoc committee resolved the problem that could have grown into a disaster over the resignation of the choir director. In our first capital funds appeal, seven families came up with advance gifts that totaled about $125,000. Their decision to do that guaranteed it would be a success. We had two men who negotiated the final price on each of those five houses we purchased. We had a fifteen-member building planning committee that made all the critical decisions on the design of the new building and on the renovation of the old church."

"I don't see how you could do all that without the vote of a congregational meeting," declared a puzzled member of the group. "I know I couldn't in my church."

"We had at least nine or ten special congregational meetings," explained the host pastor, "but those were not decision-making meetings. In each case the critical decisions had been made earlier by a relatively small number of people. Before we held a congregational meeting, we flooded the members with information. The actual meetings were held for three purposes. One was to provide a systematic overview of what was being recommended in the context of what already had been done. Thus when we met to vote to purchase that last house, the real issue we lifted up was this will now give us ownership of the entire side of this block. The second purpose was to give people a chance to ask questions. The third was formal approval of a recommended course of action. There is a big difference between making a difficult decision and formally approving a carefully prepared recommendation. The first is for a small group of people. The second is for that large group."

Four Lessons

One lesson from this story is that doers should decide, but that does oversimplify reality.

A second generalization is that with one major exception, radical change is never initiated by a majority vote. The one exception is when nearly everyone perceives the existence of a crisis, that means the status quo no longer is a tenable alternative, and a single course of action appears to be attractive to nearly everyone.

A third lesson is the vast difference between an incremental or one-step-at-a-time approach to change and sudden radical change. This pastor chose an incremental approach, which in retrospect appears to be radical change.

A fourth and more subtle lesson takes us back to the sources of authority discussed in chapter 4. Popular wisdom today insists that everyone has a right to participate in the making of any decision that will affect one's future in a significant way.[1] One way to accomplish that is to give everyone involved an equal voice. Some of us, however, prefer to give the pilot of that two-engine aircraft complete authority when one engine catches on fire while the plane is 30,000 feet off the ground and 200 miles from an airfield. Instead of asking the crew to discuss it with the passengers and give everyone an equal voice, some of us would see competence and the economy of time as sufficient sources of authority for that pilot to make a series of unilateral decisions. Likewise when those two volunteers came in with a recommended purchase price for each of those houses, it was not necessary for every member to have been actively involved in arriving at a specific dollar figure.

But Is That Democratic?

Perhaps the biggest single barrier encountered by many self-identified agents of planned change is the ideological conviction that every proposal for change must win a broad base of support before it can be implemented. This is what Harold Lindstrom advised the new minister at Grace Church. If it does not have broad-based support, it is contrary to a democratic style of decision making and may be defeated.

For many the most bitter lesson of the second half of the twentieth century has been that participatory democracy and planned change often are incompatible. The only sure way to persuade everyone that he or she has a meaningful voice in what is to be decided is to give everyone a veto. All decisions will be made only by unanimous agreement. The only thing that cannot be vetoed is the status quo. Therefore participatory democracy tends to reinforce the status quo.[2] This is less apparent in a highly homogeneous group, but almost guaranteed in a heterogeneous collection of people.

A second facet is that the desire to achieve a consensus, especially where diversity is a distinctive characteristic of the group, often means compromise and endorsing a second best or third best course of action.

This emphasis on broad-based support or a consensus also takes us back to the sources of authority. Is membership in a group to be the chief source of authority? Or should greater weight be given to competence or commitment or economy or trust or knowledge or other sources?

A simple example is the congregation that includes four hundred confirmed members. Two hundred are regular attenders. One hundred are frequent but not regular attenders at Sunday morning worship. One hundred rarely attend, partly because half of them are non-resident. One hundred sixty of the regular attenders are convinced the time has come to relocate and construct a new church building on a larger site at a better location. Together they pledge the million dollars necessary to implement that proposal. At the congregational meeting all 160 vote for relocation. Opposed are twenty of the other regular attenders, all one hundred of the irregular attenders, and eighty of those who rarely attend, some of whom have made a special trip back to oppose relocation. Twenty of the regular attenders attend, but abstain from voting. Twenty of those who rarely attend do not come to the meeting. The final vote is 160 in favor of relocation and 200 in opposition. The motion to relocate fails.

Is that a just outcome? Yes, it is if you believe membership should be the sole source of authority in decision making in that congregation.

In the case study offered earlier, the new pastor and a sufficient number of leaders concluded that competence would be superior to membership as a source of authority.

More or less unilaterally that new minister also decided that the authority of the office gave the pastor the right to conclude that a willingness to participate, not membership in that congregation, was the number-one source of authority for anyone to have a voice in designing either that new Saturday evening service for young adults or the early Sunday morning worship experience.

Who Can Conceptualize Tomorrow?

A different perspective on this question of who decides is illustrated by the skeptics and doubters who want to see before they believe. Thomas, one of the apostles, illustrated this skepticism (John 20:24-28).

That same inability to believe without seeing usually follows the successful relocation of the long-established congregation to a new and larger site and the construction of a new building.

As they walk through the new building for the first time, several of those who were either neutral or in opposition offer comments such as these, "If I had known it would be this nice, I would have voted for it." "I never dreamed we ever would have such a beautiful church!" "Why didn't we do this ten years sooner?" "I wish we had done this before our children grew up so they could enjoy it." "The old place sure looks inadequate compared to this."

These and similar comments should be accepted as expressions of natural, normal, and predictable human behavior. Many, many adults cannot conceptualize tomorrow until after they have experienced it. Similar comments are made by the liberated widow several years after her husband's death, by the individual who lived for years with a severe handicap but who now can walk comfortably after surgery for replacement of a hip joint, by some empty nest parents, and by teenagers who mourned the departure of the former youth minister but are now enthusiastic supporters of the successor.

Should the doubting Thomases who cannot conceptualize a new tomorrow be given a vote equal to those who can? That is a hard question!

Who Controls?

A third facet of this discussion on who decides was illustrated repeatedly in the case study that opened this chapter. Should the part-time organist-choir director be able to control the choice of music for that new Saturday evening service? Or should those who are designing it and who will participate in it control that decision?

The most widespread example of this is when the governing board of a congregation seeks to restrict the religious organizations to which members may contribute charitable dollars. Typically the governing board allows four to six special appeals for funds for any one church year.

The other common expression of this control question is the unified budget. People are asked to contribute to one budget that covers all approved needs. The budget committee or the governing board will allocate all contributions among the various needs. The dream was this would place a floor under giving. In fact, it has placed a ceiling over giving. A rapidly growing number of people want a voice in determing where their charitable dollars will end up. They prefer designated giving to the unified budget.[3]

What Is the Issue?

The central issue here for the agent of planned change initiated from within an organization is easy to state, but difficult to resolve.

To return to the opening illustration, are you convinced, as Harold Lindstrom was, that every proposed change must have a broad base of support?

Or are you comfortable with the style of that impatient young minister who operated on the assumption that the required support was only that needed to turn an idea into reality?

Should control be vested largely in those who hold official positions of influence? Or should control rest largely with those who share the dream and are eager to venture into a new tomorrow?

Your answers to those questions will influence your choice of a strategy for change.

Chapter Six

What Is Your Strategy?

During the late 1980s and early 1990s, discontent with the costs and the coverage of health care in the United States became one of the two or three top domestic issues. Nearly everyone—including politicians, patients, pastors, physicians, hospital administrators, social workers, labor union leaders, Democrats, Republicans, denominational leaders, governors, executives of large manufacturing corporations, and other employers—expressed discontent with the present system.

If broad-based discontent is the key to planned change, why was the Congress so slow to act? The answer, of course, is that it was impossible to rally the political support required to adopt any one course of action.

Three Levels of Change

Why was it so difficult to reach agreement on a course of action when the discontent was so deep and so broad? One part of the explanation was the absence of agreement on how much change was needed. The national debate was being conducted at three levels. One group of discontented advocates for change simply wanted to tinker with the existing system by controlling costs and improving quality. A second group focused on a more complex proposal for change. They wanted to broaden coverage so that everyone would have easy access to decent health care, to control costs, to reduce administrative overhead, and yet to maintain a high level of quality. The tradeoff for that broad goal, as the state legislature in Oregon recognized, would be some form of rationing of exceptionally expensive health care procedures. A third group advocated a more radical change. They wanted to scrap the present system and replace it with a national health insurance program similar to that in effect in Canada.

Together these three groups of discontented people represented a substantial majority of the American population as well as a majority in the Congress. The lack of a consensus for change was not because of an absence of discontent. The problem was the absence of a majority for one specific course of action. One group wanted modest changes. A second wanted substantial changes. The third group wanted radical change. No one group could rally a majority.

This debate over health care introduces one of the fundamental issues in planned change. How much change is needed? Does this proposal call for first level changes? This usually means continuing to do what we are now doing, only better. One example of a first level change is to improve the public schools by increasing the financing.

The second level of change is more complicated. This might involve changing the system for recruiting and training teachers or combining kindergarten and first and second grade in one room to replace the old closely graded system. A second level change in Sunday school would be to switch from one class of five to ten children with one teacher for each grade to a team of three to five teachers with twenty-five to forty students in one big room.

Radical or third level change calls for big departures from the status quo. Instead of remodeling or constructing an addition to the old building, the congregation decides to relocate. Instead of tinkering with the public school system, every pupil receives a voucher good for full tuition to a school of that pupil's choice. Instead of expanding Medicare and Medicaid, the third level change is to adopt a national health insurance program. Instead of going to a marriage enrichment weekend (first level) or seeking the advice of a marriage counselor (second level), the couple decides to get a divorce.

First level changes usually encounter fewer obstacles and require a less sophisticated strategy than do proposals for the more disruptive third level changes.

A Five Step Sequence

Planned change initiated from within does not happen unless a substantial degree of discontent with the status quo exists. That is the first step. Frequently a useful means of broadening that base of discontent is to help others identify the discrepancy between the vision of a new tomorrow and contemporary reality.

One alternative available to only a few of us normal mortals is the impact of the magnetic and deeply respected leader described in chapter 1. A second is the arrival of the remarkably competent and visionary benevolent dictator described in chapter 2. A third is the relatively colorless, purposeful, determined, patient, and persistent plodder who comes in and changes the game by changing the players. Three or four years later nearly every officer or volunteer leader or staff member is the handpicked choice of that new leader. The new broom sweeps clean, and institutional resistance is eliminated by replacing most of the resisters, promoting a couple to different positions where they are newcomers with no accrued power, and winning over as converts those who are open to a fresh approach. For this alternative to have transformational long-term results normally requires ten to fifteen years in that office for that leader.

This is a strategy that has been followed by regional bishops and their counterparts in other traditions. Five years after election, they have the benefit of a large number of cooperative allies. In a few cases the non-cooperative pastors have been encouraged or persuaded to move to another regional judicatory or to another denomination or to leave the ministry. A few years later most of the volunteer leaders are members who joined since the arrival of that new leader. Many of the long-time resisters feel frustrated, ignored, disenfranchised, and powerless. One reason they feel that way is that after years on the "winning" side whenever change was proposed, they are now on the losing side.

In a congregational setting this process can be facilitated by bringing in a flood of new members. The new pastor often feels frustrated by the resistance of the many long-term members who repeatedly refer back to "the good old days." Instead of seeking to build a new leadership cadre out of yesterday's members, the new pastor concentrates on enlisting scores of new members.

A completely different approach to broadening the base of discontent is to take a group of leaders from this long established congregation to visit another parish which, five years ago, resembled this one. Today, however, that church to be visited resembles the dream of what this parish could be in the future.

The visitors see a real-life version of tomorrow and compare it with the back-home reality. This self-identified discrepancy between what is and what could be stirs up discontent with the status quo. (See chapter 3 for an elaboration of this concept.)

That Crucial Second Step

After the advocate of planned change has enlisted supportive allies who also are discontented with the status quo comes that crucial second step. This is the creation of the initiating group, which will design a specific course of action.

The wise advocate of change will recognize this may be far more difficult than it first appears.

Five facets of this second step illustrate the complexity. One was illustrated by the debate over health care in the United States. Will the best solution require only minor changes or substantial change or radical change? Which level of change are you advocating as you design a course of action?

Equally critical is the question of who will do this? Those who are most discontented? Or will everyone in this original initiating group be given an equal voice? Or will this process include inviting other respected and influential leaders who are not especially discontented to come in and help to shape the recommendation?

A third factor is time. Will the emphasis be on fast action? Or on involving more people? Or on a more thorough indepth analysis by the few who are prepared to invest the amount of time and energy needed?

Each of these three alternatives carries predictable results. The decision to move as fast as possible in bringing this to a final decision greatly increases the risk of rejection by the governing board or by the congregation.

The decision to broaden the base of participation usually will enlarge the number of people who favor change. That runs the risk, however, of changing the focus to find the compromise that can win the largest number of supporters. Frequently this results in a cosmetic or first level change that only postpones dealing with the basic problem.

This often is illustrated by the congregation in which 40 percent of the members favor remodeling the ancient building, 30 percent support construction of a new wing, and 20 percent want to relocate. The search for an acceptable compromise may produce a decision to remodel. Or it may result in a compromise that calls for construction of an addition to what is in fact an obsolete building on an inadequate site at a poor location. Six years later the congregation votes to relocate.

The decision to encourage a few discontented people to spend far more time in a more thorough analysis often alienates that group from the rest of the people. To use the previous example, suppose this study group comes up with a unanimous decision to recommend relocation. That recommendation goes to a congregational meeting for a decision and is rejected by a 70 to 30 margin.

The fourth factor is one few initiators of planned change believe to be possible. Expansion of the size of the initiating group to include people beyond the original circle of discontent can result in the enlistment of creative individuals who will suggest a better quality course of action than any of the original circle had ever contemplated! This may be an improvement on the original design or it may be a substantially different action plan. Are you open to constructive suggestions from latecomers?

Finally, who is the audience for this recommended course of

action? Will it be directed to a standing committee? If that is the client, consider two alternative scenarios. The preferable one is to bring a few members of that standing committee into the initiating group as early as possible. Broaden the participation base. Share ownership, minimize surprises. The alternative scenario may be rejection. Standing committees normally are cemeteries for new ideas originated outside that standing committee.

Is the governing board the primary audience? If so, it often will be wise to offer the board at least two preliminary progress reports before submitting the final recommendation. If it is anticipated the final report will call for substantial or second level changes, it usually is wiser to submit at least three progress reports spaced a month or two apart. If the final recommendation will propose more radical or third level changes, at least four earlier progress reports may be advisable. The goal is to avoid surprises. Experience suggests that surprises often evoke hostile responses. This is especially likely if the recommendation calls for second or third level changes.

If the primary audience for the recommendation to come from this initiating group is expected to be a newly created ad hoc action task force charged with implementing that recommendation, a different set of expectations emerge. First, expect this to be a receptive action-oriented group. Second, encourage the inclusion of two or three people from the initiating group on this action task force. That often helps to preserve the integrity and internal coherence of the original proposal for change. Third, the higher the level of competence of the members of that task force, the more likely they will feel free to amend, enlarge, or alter the basic recommendation they have been asked to implement. (This is a common example: The task force is directed to find a ten acre parcel within five miles of the present meeting place as the relocation site. They purchase a fifteen acre parcel of land seven miles away.)

If the number-one audience for this recommendation is submitted to the entire membership at a congregational meeting, the process should be redefined. Ideally every interested board, group, class, committee, commission, and organization should have had the opportunity to receive and discuss the recommendation before it comes before that congregational meeting. This may be of critical importance if this recommendation is for third level change. The three basic generalizations to guide this process are (1) normal people tend to be more receptive to a new idea when it is no longer new, (2) normal adults often need time to talk themselves into accepting change, and (3) the vote at the congregational meeting should not be sought until every leader is reasonably confident on what the outcome will be.

This discussion leads into the third step in the process of planned change initiated from within an organization.

That Often Overlooked Third Step

Impatient advocates of change are tempted to move from discontent to creating an initiating group that produces a recommendation for change to seeking approval or adoption of their proposal. Often this is the road to rejection. The reason is this sequence overlooks the need to build a support group for the proposed change.

The smaller the circle of discontent and/or the more radical (third level) the proposed change and/or the smaller the initiating group and/or the shorter the time frame for discussion, the more likely the omission of this third step will result in rejection.

A few of the potential components of the support group were identified earlier in the discussions on expanding the circle of discontent and on audiences or clients for this proposed new course of action (chapter 3).

If adoption will require votes, the expansion of the support group should include voters. If implementation will require money or designated contributions, that should be one part of the creation of this support group. If a board or committee or officer or individual possesses the power to veto the new idea, an effort should be made no later than creation of the support group to enlist support from that potential veto source. If support is impossible to achieve, a compromise goal may be passive neutrality.

A substantially different approach to this step is illustrated by those leaders who abhor any tactic that could be described as "political." They pray for their opponents; they seek to be faithful and obedient servants of the Lord; they always try to be open to the power of the Holy Spirit; they display a completely open and trusting personality; they often excel in one-to-one relationships; and they gradually become the spiritual mentors of an increasing number of influential leaders in that organization. Their profound and unwavering Christian commitment earns for them the trust and loyalty of people. The resisters who place a higher priority on yesterday and on tradition than on Christian commitment see their influence eroding. Eventually—and this usually means years, not months—this model of a Christ-centered and highly disciplined leader wins the converts necessary to overcome the resistance to change.

A completely different approach to building support and to overcoming opposition is illustrated by the charismatic leader who comes in and builds a large and informal network of enthusiastic followers. Together they simply overwhelm the resisters by the combination of numbers, optimism, enthusiasm, vigor, prayer, commitment, persistence, and future-orientation.

The Fourth Step

The fourth in this five-step process is approval and implementation. This raises two subtle and overlapping questions.

First, is it really necessary to secure congregational approval for this proposed change? A general answer is not for first level changes, maybe for second level, and almost always for third level changes. Adding a part-time secretary to the staff usually is a first level change and can be implemented by the personnel committee and the finance committee. Adding and calling a second full-time pastor usually will be perceived as third level change. Typically that requires congregational approval first for creating the new position and subsequently to extend a call to the new pastor.

The pastor in the case study in the previous chapter initiated many changes, but each was widely perceived as first or second level change, so it was not necessary to seek congregational approval. Instead that pastor worked diligently to avoid the withholding of permission. That pastor operated on a sound principle of planned change. The result was a large number of first and second level changes eventually added up to third level transformation. Whenever possible make changes by addition, not by subtraction.

That generalization introduces the second question on implementation. Who will be affected by this change? A proposal to remove the partition dividing those two small second floor Sunday school rooms will affect only a few. That is a first level change. The absence of opposition plus the resources required to do it may be all that is required for implementation.

The proposal to expand the Sunday morning schedule by adding an early worship service will be viewed by most who never attend it as a first level change—unless it requires a change in the entire Sunday morning schedule. If many of the regular attenders have to change their personal Sunday morning schedule, they will tend to view this as a second level change. The most obvious example consists of the five members of the chancel choir that used to sing at ten-thirty and now sing at eleven, but those five leave the chancel choir to become the nucleus for a new choir with a new director and a different selection of anthems that will sing at eight-thirty. For those five choir members, this may be perceived as a third level change.

Therefore, these five choir members, and perhaps the new director, have a right to expect to have a voice in designing that new early worship experience. Their approval and support is necessary for implementation of this third level change to create a new and different worship experience.

The other dozen choir members, however, probably will view the half-hour change in their schedule as either a first level or second level change.

As a broad generalization those who perceive the proposed course of action to represent a third level of change in their lives have a right to expect their approval will be sought. Those who will be unaffected, or who perceive this to be a first level change, probably will not be offended if their approval is not sought.

The Fifth Step

The new pastor announces that a cooperative design has been prepared that calls for this and two nearby congregations to offer a special Ascension Day worship service the second Thursday in May. The new pastor's congregation has never celebrated Ascension Day in its entire history. No one opposes it, partly because they do not want to expose their ignorance, partly because they do not want to be perceived as pagans. This congregation averages a little over a hundred at Sunday morning worship. To the pastor's surprise and delight, sixty parishioners appear for this special service that is being held in one of the two cooperative churches' sanctuary. The pastor's private hope had been thirty.

A new idea had been initiated and implemented. Should we continue this cooperative venture next year?

That introduces the fifth step in this sequence. Which changes are institutionalized as permanent? Which ones are implemented once, but not institutionalized?

During the eight-month vacancy period between pastors at First Church, a total of seventeen different individuals filled the pulpit on Sunday mornings. Four preach on three or four occasions. None of the four is ever installed, however.

Eventually a new pastor is called and arrives. On the third Sunday of the new minister's tenure, an elaborate installation is held with two denominational executives and a couple of other pastors assisting.

The role of those visiting preachers is never institutionalized, but the new "permanent" pastor is installed in a memorable ceremony. The visiting preachers represent change, but no one is prepared to institutionalize their role. The symbolism of that installation ceremony is viewed as important in institutionalizing the role of the called minister.

Another example is the widespread pattern of "cutting back"

on the Sunday morning schedule to only one worship service for July and August. This change is seen as temporary and often receives little discussion. It is a temporary change and will not be institutionalized.

If, however, in late October someone proposes that the schedule be reduced from two services on Sunday morning to only one, beginning with the first Sunday in January, that probably will evoke widespread comments and considerable opposition. Why? Because most will view this as a permanent change.

In many cases a specific proposal for change is for one time only and thus is relatively easy to implement. If, however, it represents a permanent departure from the status quo, and thus must be institutionalized, far more care and much more work must be given to implementation.

With three exceptions this five-step sequence represents a widely used strategy for planned change initiated from within an organization. One exception is the widely perceived crisis that changes the rules completely. A second exception is the benevolent dictator who is able to impose changes unilaterally. The third exception is the charismatic individual who replaces this sequence with the power of that magnetic personality.

For most initiators of planned change, the pressure of time prohibits waiting for the crisis, the role of the benevolent dictator is either unavailable or unacceptable, and others do not view them as charismatic leaders. What do they do? The first step may be to adapt this five-step strategy to that situation. The second may be to look at tactics or simply to review a checklist of guidelines for change.

A Checklist for Change Agents

What are the guidelines that enable one to function effectively as an agent of planned change initiated from within an organization? (A few of these were discussed briefly in chapter 2.) Here are several guidelines that may strengthen your tactics and make it easier to implement your strategy.

1. *Earn trust.* Do not rely on the authority of the office to con-

fer trust. Whether it is the newly elected director of a para-church organization or a recently arrived denominational executive or a new pastor, the first priority is to win the confidence of the people. Earn the right to be trusted.

2. *Life is relational.* Build relationships with potential future allies. Identify and build relationships with potential future opponents. Rational leaders urge, "Trust the process!" Relational leaders intuitively know that the primary level of trust is personal. Friends and acquaintances listen more openly to proposals for change than do strangers.

3. *Ask questions.* More can be learned by asking questions and listening than by talking.[1]

4. *Define the issue.* This may be the most critical guideline on this list. The beginning point is leaders should accept the responsibility for stating the question. Whoever frames the issues influences how people will respond.

One example is that too often after it has been agreed that the status quo no longer is a viable alternative, someone defines the issue as a choice between the status quo and change. Since most people naturally will prefer the status quo if offered as one option, that loads the question against change. A common way for that to happen is to let a means-to-an-end question (schedule, budget, use of the property, staffing, building maintenance, etc.) become the dominant issue. (See chapter 8 for one example of this.)

The skilled advocate of planned change places a high priority on defining the central issue in terms of ministry, role, purpose, and goals rather than as a means-to-an-end question. A simple example is the congregation meeting in an obsolete or deteriorating building on an inadequate site at a poor location. The issue should not be stated as relocation versus remaining at this site. That loads the question in favor of perpetuating the status quo. One possibility would be, "Do you favor spending $2 million for the renovation of this building and the acquisition of additional land or spending $2 million to buy a larger site at a better location and construct a new building?" Another might be, "Do you prefer continuing in this building at this site and watching our congregation grow older and smaller or do you favor a fresh start for a new era at another location?"

In other words, it often is both more realistic and positive to propose that the choices are between Change A and Change B. Do not offer the status quo as a viable alternative if that is not true.

Furthermore, the issue should be stated in a manner that will enable people to discern quickly and easily whether this proposal calls for first level change, second level change, or third level change. Proposals for third level change are far more likely to arouse immediate opposition than are recommendations for first level change. Third level change also requires a more sophisticated strategy and a more varied support group.

It is both tempting and easy for an opponent to define the issue in words that will evoke widespread hostility. It is always better to define the issue as early as possible in terms that place the proposed change in a favorable light.

5. *Count only the yes votes.* For many first level changes and for some second level changes, it is not necessary to secure either approval or permission. All that is necessary are (a) the withholding of disapproval and (b) the support of those who will make it happen.

Thus the pastor may say to the governing board, "As of this morning thirty-one young adults have told me they would be interested in participating in a Saturday evening worship service if we offered it. Unless some of you object, we hope to be able to begin worshiping together on the second Saturday evening in March. We will keep you informed on what happens."

The father of one of the young men who will be involved gives an enthusiastic endorsement of both the idea and of the pastor's initiative. No one else on the board voices either approval or disapproval beyond asking a couple of simple questions. The proposal carries with 33 yes votes (the pastor's, the father's, and 31 young adults') and no dissent.

6. *Affirm tradition.* One way of placing the proposed change in a favorable light is to identify and affirm local traditions that are consistent with and supportive of the proposal.

"This congregation was organized in 1926 to reach newcomers

to this neighborhood. The proposal for a second worship service on Sunday morning is consistent with our tradition to reach and serve the people moving into this community."

7. *Build on strengths.* Identify and affirm strengths, resources, and assets as foundations on which to launch this new ministry. "Our congregation includes three families with developmentally disabled children, that means we not only are faced with a need, we also have sensitive, concerned, and knowledgeable parents who will be able to help implement this proposal for a new Sunday school class for developmentally disabled people."

8. *Concentrate on one-at-a-time.* Whenever possible, choose the route of incremental change. If the goal is to expand the women's organization, it may be wise to add one circle every year, or perhaps every six months, rather than attempt to completely restructure that entire organization.[2]

9. *Use addition, not subtraction.* Whenever possible, add to the existing schedule, organization, or group life. Concentrate on giving birth to new classes, groups, circles, or choirs, rather than seeking to reform the old.

10. *Identify legitimatizers.* Identify those widely respected and influential leaders who, by their support, can lend credibility and legitimacy to the proposal for change. Enlist these legitimatizers as early as possible in your initiating group.

11. *Identify potential support groups.* Identify the organizations, classes, committees, and other groups that might be interested in participating in a coalition for change.

12. *Identify potential opponents early.* When allowed to fret in isolation, potential opponents often turn into diehard antagonists. If they are identified early, a few may be persuaded to become allies in pioneering a new tomorrow and others may choose the option of passive neutrality.

13. *Rally the cheerleaders.* The agent of change may be the number-one advocate for a particular course of action, but that often is not sufficient. Identify potential supporters who will speak a good word for the proposed change to their spouses, parents, friends, neighbors, relatives, colleagues at work, and adult children. This often is a crucial component of that third step of creating a broad-based support group. Do it early!

14. *Give people time.* Err on the side of patience. Give people the time many will need to talk themselves into supporting the proposed change.

15. *Avoid surprises!* The natural and predictable response to an unexpected recommendation for change is to reject it. Do not surprise people.

16. *Decide between permission and approval.* For many changes, approval of the entire organization is not necessary. All that is needed is either (a) permission to go ahead or (b) the withholding of disapproval. See this as a spectrum with approval at one end, disapproval at the other end, permission next to approval, and the withholding of disapproval next to disapproval. Most teenagers use that four-point spectrum in relationships with their parents. Frequently the withholding of disapproval is an acceptable and attainable level of permission for first level changes. Permission usually is needed for second level changes and approval for third level changes.

17. *Define the level.* Frequently the initiator of planned change is tempted, often by the urgency of the need, to understate the degree of change required. Third level changes are perceived to be only second level while second level changes are offered in the guise of first level.

The charismatic leader or the benevolent dictator may be able to implement change by understating the level. For the remaining 95 percent of all leaders, however, that often is the road to rejection and frustration.

A better approach is to measure the degree of change from the perspective of those who will be most affected by this break with the status quo. The new member who joins the relocated congregation two years after completion of the first building does not see that relocation as radical change. The seventy-one-year-old widow who lives across the street from the former meeting place, where she was married forty-six years ago, perceives relocation to be a radical departure from the status quo.

18. *Create ad hoc study committees.* Standing committees usually are comfortable with first level changes initiated from within that committee. If, however, the need is for second level, and for all third level changes, do not expect a standing committee to be

the initiating group called for in the second step of the five-part strategy. That is an unreasonable expectation! The one exception is when a standing committee is confronted with what is an undeniable crisis. Use ad hoc study committees to initiate and ad hoc action committees or task forces to implement.

19. *Emphasize redundant communication.* One of the most effective means of minimizing unnecessary opposition is to keep everyone as well informed as possible about both the definition of the problem and the proposed alternative responses.

20. *Begin with winners.* Proponents of change often are confronted with three choices, (a) the change that is most urgent, (b) the change that is essential to implementation of a long-term strategy, and (c) the change that is most likely to be the easiest to implement. Whenever possible, begin with the third. Create a success story. Build momentum. Win allies who become more committed to change with victories. Move up the learning curve from a low beginning point. That high fourth hurdle will not appear to be as high after first jumping over three lower hurdles.

21. *Use temporary systems.* As was pointed out earlier, the resistance usually is less to a change that is perceived to be temporary than it is to permanent change. Therefore, when it is honestly possible, some changes should be proposed as a temporary course of action. "None of us are wise enough to know how this will turn out, so we cannot evaluate the proposal until after we have tried it. After we see what happens, we can determine whether we want this to be permanent or whether we will return to the old system."

22. *Affirm stability zones.* All normal human beings need a degree of predictability and stability in our lives. Whether it be the bed we sleep in or the hour we eat dinner or the place where we worship on Sunday morning or the chair we sit in at the table or the station we turn to for the evening news, we all prefer continuity and stability.[3]

Therefore, identify and affirm the stability zones that will be perpetuated. This may be the Sunday morning schedule or a circle in the women's organization or an adult Sunday school class or the priority given to missions or the use of familiar hymns.

Undergird proposals for changes by affirming many stability zones for as many people as possible.

23. *Mandated change is different.* Occasionally an organization is required by external forces to make changes. One came when the United States Congress declared the military academies must admit female cadets beginning with the entering class of 1976. Other mandated changes may come from local governments, denominational headquarters, or some other external force. If and when that occurs, recognize that mandates change the rulebook. People react differently than anticipated to externally mandated changes.[4]

24. *Do not accept a defeat as final.* Recall the useful bit of ancient wisdom that advises the only important battle in a war is the last one. Many changes become possible only after a proposal has been rejected at least once. (One example is the third scenario in chapter 8.)

The overwhelming majority of congregations that implemented a recommendation to relocate the meeting place did so only after rejecting relocation on one or more occasions. Many of the most effective pastors returned a call to that parish once or twice before accepting it. The world would be filled with bachelors if the first rejection of a proposal of marriage had been accepted as the final word.

Patience and persistence rank up there with trust, vision, and competence as among the most valuable characteristics of the effective agent of planned change.

25. *When necessary, change the players.* This is placed last because it should be seen as a last resort. Occasionally, however, the agent of change will be immobilized until someone is replaced in a crucial leadership position. This may be the person chairing a critical committee, a program staff member, a bishop, a senior minister, a treasurer, or a choir director.

If the need is to play a new game, it often is necessary to recruit new players. The old players often are tempted to want to play the old game.

Chapter Seven

Reform or Create?

Several of my friends couldn't understand why, at my age, I would accept a call to go out and plant a new mission," explained the fifty-nine-year-old mission developer of a new, four-year-old congregation that was averaging nearly six hundred at worship. "I told them that, after nearly three decades as a parish pastor, I thought I had mastered nearly all the skills I needed except one. That one exception was how to persuade the leaders of churches of the need for change. My first pastorate lasted seven years. I left when I finally recognized that three of the key leaders were unalterably opposed to relocation. During those seven years our attendance had grown from a little over a hundred at one Sunday morning service to nearly three hundred at two services plus another sixty at a new Saturday evening service we had started. The building was obsolete. The site was small and hemmed in by big apartment buildings, and we had a total of thirty offstreet parking spaces. We couldn't grow any more at that location, but those three men blocked every proposal to relocate.

"My second pastorate was in a racially changing neighborhood, and I got shot down when I tried to integrate that congregation," continued this pastor, "so I left after three frustration-filled years. My last pastorate was the most fun of the three. I came to an old First Church-type of congregation that had peaked in size in 1955 and then went through four senior ministers and fifteen years of numerical decline. When I came in 1970, they were averaging less than two hundred at worship. When I left, we were averaging nearly six hundred in worship and well over half that number in Sunday school. My first defeat came when I lost on a proposal to add a church nurse to the staff in 1985. The opposition claimed that a staff nurse would reinforce our image as an aging congregation. My next defeat was a proposal to hire a musician who would organize a band that would provide the music for an alternative service in the fellowship hall at the same time we had our traditional service in the sanctuary at eleven o'clock Sunday morning. I thought that would be a great way to reach the nineteen- to twenty-two-year-old age groups which weren't going to church anywhere. We had an associate minister who was eager to organize and lead that service, but we were shot down by the traditionalists. My third defeat came when I proposed we open a Christian day school for kids age four through nine.

"So, when the call came to organize a new mission, I took it," concluded this happy pastor. "It meant a $30,000 cut in my compensation package, but I've more than made that up in satisfactions. Besides that, my salary next year will be almost what it was in my last year in that church."

*   *   *

"We tried to persuade the local Council of Churches to hire a church planner who would be available to work with congregations and the local regional judicatories," recalled a denominational executive. "Their board, however, was so concerned with their budget problems and two incompetent staff persons, who no one had the guts to fire, that they wouldn't listen to us. We guaranteed the funds to finance that position for the first two years on the assumption that by the third year, it would be self-supporting from user fees, but they wouldn't cooperate. So we started our own separate cooperative church planning agency that now is in its seventh year and reports a financial surplus at the end of every fiscal year. We decided it would be easier and quicker to create the new rather than to try to reform the old."

* * *

"I taught in the public school system here for eleven years until I couldn't put up with the incompetence of the people in the headquarters office," explained the director of a private Christian school for three year olds through grade four. "The system had deteriorated to the point that the priorities were to meet the needs of the administrators first, the janitors second, the bus drivers third, the teachers fourth, and the children fifth. I worked with six different principals in eleven years in an effort to reform the system. Finally, I gave up when leaders from these five churches came to me and asked if I would organize and supervise a new school that would be sponsored by these five congregations. This looked like a chance to turn my vision of what a school should be into reality. It is now seven years later, and we have a great school with an enrollment of 135 including the nursery and kindergarten, an exceptional faculty, wonderful support from the parents, and a great bunch of children. I've worked harder than I ever did before in my life, but I've also gained a lifetime of satisfactions in these seven years. It sure is a lot more fun to create the new than to try to reform the old!"

* * *

These three comments illustrate a fork in the road that has confronted thousands of agents of change. The list includes Martin Luther, John Wesley, Norman Thomas, Franklin D. Roosevelt, Martin Luther King, Jr., Thomas A. Edison, and scores of pastors who left the security of a denominational system to go out and organize a new independent church.

What Are Your Assumptions?

One group of change agents is guided by several assumptions including these three:

1. People can change.
2. Systems can be changed.
3. A committed minority can prevail over a passive majority.

These individuals also carry a deep institutional loyalty to that organization. Therefore they seek to change or reform that organization by working from within. While they may be impatient personalities, they recognize the merits of patience, persistence, and tenacity. Most would rank higher on the scale that measures loyalty than on the scale that defines the entrepreneurial personality.

By contrast, those who prefer to create the new rather than to persist in efforts to reform the old tend to place a relatively low value on institutional loyalties, they are convinced the call is for action now, and they tend to be impatient personalities.

In American Christianity these are the people who went out and launched what became a new denomination or a new parachurch organization.

In American politics these are the political figures who launched what became a third party. Theodore Roosevelt, Norman Thomas, John Anderson, and Eugene McCarthy are examples from the twentieth century.

In American business these are the entrepreneurs who went out and organized a new company. J. C. Penney, Bill Gates, Sam Walton, and Ted Turner are examples.

What Are the Choices?

The person who is discontented with the status quo in any institution or organization has five choices. One is to seek to be a reformer and work at making what are perceived to be the needed changes from within. The officeholders sometimes refer to them as "the loyal opposition."

A second is to continue as a member, but to minimize the sense of frustration by finding a new outlet for one's creativity, energy, commitment, time, enthusiasm, money, and skill. One example of this is those millions of Americans who continue as members of the same congregation they have been in for many years, but worship in another church on Saturday evening or early Sunday morning or on Sunday evening. A second example is the frustrated church member who devotes a huge chunk of time, money, and energy to a parachurch organization. A third example is the member who is discontented with the new pastor and now rarely attends worship but is the number-one pillar of an adult Sunday school class. A fourth example is the minister who once was active in seeking to reform that denomination, but now devotes that time and energy to a new cooperative interchurch venture.

A third choice for that person who is deeply discontented with the status quo is to simply drop out. One highly visible example in North America is that huge number of Roman Catholic priests who have dropped out to marry and rear a family while pursuing a secular vocation, but continuing as active Catholic worshipers.

A fourth alternative is to leave and unite with another institution. This is a long list and includes attorneys who have switched to another law firm, ministers who have changed denominations, voters who have switched political parties, church members who have left one congregation to join another (this is an especially common pattern among churchgoers born after World War II), educators who leave the large central city school system to teach in a private school at a lower salary, Roman Catholic nuns who have united with a Protestant congregation, and frustrated university professors who leave to teach in what they believe will be a more sympathetic and supportive environment.

The fifth alternative is to go out and create the new. These impatient people cannot continue to function within the organization that successfully resists reform, they are not ready to drop into inactivity, they will not drop out completely, and they do not see much merit in switching their allegiance to another long-established institution.

The most highly visible examples consist of those adults born in the first four decades of this century who spent many years as loyal pillars in a Protestant congregation founded before 1960. Increasingly frustrated after years of efforts directed to reforming that congregation or denomination, they drop out to help pioneer a new independent or nondenominational church designed to reach and serve people born after 1955.

The combination of discontent with the status quo, commitment to a vision of what could be, impatience, optimism, energy, and a venturesome spirit lead to the decision to go out and create the new. The result may be a new alternative school for those children who are not being well served by the public schools. It may lead to a new law firm committed to environmental reform. It may produce a new parachurch organization committed to creative responses to the needs of the staff of very large churches. It may result in the creation of a new publishing house or a new music group or a new adult Sunday school class or a new parachurch youth movement or a new hospice for people living with AIDS or a new Saturday evening worship service or a new congregation.

Sooner or later most of those who become severely discontented with the institutional status quo are confronted with this fork in the road. Do I remain here and persist in seeking to reform this organization from within? Or do I leave to create that which will enable my dreams to become reality?

The patient and persistent agent of planned change who is committed to reform continues to work from within. The impatient visionary leaves to create the new. The tradeoff is between institutional loyalty and impatience. The stronger motivating force usually determines the outcome.

Who Are the Victims?

Perhaps the most unfortunate victims of this choice between seeking to reform the old or going out to create the new are the reformers who stay with the old. Their diagnosis of the problem was accurate, their prescription was a perfect response to that diagnosis, but they lacked the allies required to make that prescription work. Those potential allies had left to go out and help give birth to the new. The reformers look back on a life filled with hope, faithfulness, patience, loyalty, and disappointments while their departed friends enjoy the fruits of impatience, creativity, action, and helping to pioneer the new.

Chapter Eight

Three Scenarios

My predecessor clearly was a poor match for this congregation, and he left after two years," explained the newly arrived pastor of the ninety-three-year-old Hope Church. "He's an introverted personality who likes to read, to go to conferences, and to volunteer for denominational responsibilities; but apparently he never really enjoyed the parish ministry. He left here to go to graduate school. During his tenure the worship attendance here dropped from an average of 135 on Sunday morning to about 90. Since I came here in June, the attendance has climbed back up to where we're now averaging about 100 to 115, but that may be the peak unless we can attract a flood of new members. Most of our members were born back in the first third of the twentieth century, and they like the status quo. Our Sunday school averages less than sixty in attendance, and half of those are in the two adult classes, both of which were organized shortly after World War II. Our women's fellowship has two circles, both meeting in the afternoon, and both are composed largely of women past sixty. We have a half dozen high school kids, and I meet with them twice a month, but they come more out of loyalty to me than anything else."

"What do you, as a minister, do best?" asked the visitor from denominational headquarters, who had stopped by at the request of this thirty-nine-year-old pastor.

"Preach, teach, and work with people," came the immediate response. "While I'm not the best pulpiteer in the world, at every place I've served, the people told me they appreciated my preaching, and that's true here also. I'm told they felt my predecessor's sermons were over their heads, and my sermons give them something to think about. I think the two reasons the attendance has rebounded since I came are my preaching and the fact that I've now called in every home at least once."

"That makes sense," observed the denominational staffer. "What do the people want to happen next?"

"That's part of my problem" replied the pastor. "I think the answer is either to return to the good old days of 1960 or nothing. I keep telling them I need their direction, but I don't get any creative response. What should I do?"

The easiest choice might be to settle in as the resident chaplain for a couple of years, rebuild the institutional strength, and, after a total of perhaps four years, move on to a more challenging assignment. In some traditions that is a more tempting alternative than it is in others.

A more promising alternative could be to combine this minister's self-identified three strengths of "preach, teach, and work with people" with a strategy of incremental change. During those first several months of calling on every household, this newly arrived pastor could conclude every visit with two questions. "What do you think should be our top priority in ministry during the next few years?"

Typically, this will evoke such responses as, "Do more with our youth" or "Rebuild our church attendance back up to where it used to be" or "Reach more younger families." When the minister hears the suggestion that appears the most promising, the second question is raised, "Who do you think could be our best allies in making that happen?"

Thus the subtle seeds of discontent with the status quo are sown concurrrently with an effort to identify allies for that initiating group.

A few months later the new minister challenges the members of the governing board, all of whom have been visited at least twice by the pastor and several have expressed some discontent with those two previous years of watching the congregation grow older.

"Would you like to see this congregation grow younger? I am convinced it can happen here! To make that happen, however, will require a few modest changes. We will have to strengthen the Sunday school, expand the program, and maybe even add an early service. I will need to be free to spend the equivalent of a couple of days a week on that, and we will need a little additional money for programming. What do you think? Should we give it a try?"

The minister makes it clear that no decision is expected at this meeting. While that suggestion is circulating on the grapevine for another month or two or three, the new minister uses this time to discuss it in greater detail with (a) potential allies, (b) potential future supporters, and (c) potential future opponents. When it comes before the governing board the next time, the pastor (1) listens for and processes constructive suggestions for improvement of the proposal, (2) identifies and enlists allies who will be volunteer workers when the time comes, and (c) solicits promises of designated second-mile financial contributions from those members who support the idea, but won't lift a hand (except perhaps to sign a check) to turn the dream into reality.

At that third or fourth meeting of the governing board when formal approval is sought, the wording of the motion should be as general as possible, perhaps "to encourage our minister to attract more young families and to support those changes that will be necessary to help cause this to happen, as long as it does not require changes in the budget."

The basic goal is to attract a new generation around the focus of helping to pioneer a new worship experience with families that include children.

The process of implementation parallels the concept of "networking" in organizing a new congregation. The minister identifies the already existing networks of younger families in that community and seeks to enlist one or more active allies from each of those networks. The first action step may be creation of a Bible study group that meets in the home of a couple who are part of a network of people who "haven't gotten around yet to getting back into church." The second step in this sequence of incremental change might be a "Mothers' Day Out" cooperative childcare program from 9:00 A.M. to 3:00 P.M. every Tuesday, at the church.

Within a few more months several families out of these networks are attending Sunday morning. The noisy children are seen as disruptive by some of the oldtimers, but at least a few make them feel welcome.

Shortly thereafter the minister enlists several of these adults plus a few others who are still out on the fringe to design a 5:00 P.M. Saturday worship service for families with young children. That hour is chosen for the benefit of the children—and their parents—who still enjoy an afternoon nap, but it is early enough not to interfere with a late Saturday evening meal. Those who are interested are invited to stay and eat the evening meal together. Several adults also remain to help pioneer a new Saturday evening Bible study group (or parenting class). Three longtime members, all grandmothers, have been enlisted to staff the Saturday evening childcare. They meet and make new friends from among these newcomers. These three grandmothers also become the leading cheerleaders for the new Saturday evening service and, when needed, serve as blocking backs when the pastor runs the next new idea before the governing board.

Four years later an early Sunday morning service is added to the schedule as many of the babies are now old enough to be in Sunday school. (The four largest classes of first graders in the United States during the last three decades of the twentieth century are the entering classes in the fall of 1970, 1995, 1996, and 1998.)

Ten years later one of the oldtimers reflects, "You know, I don't recall that we ever voted on it, but this church is larger today than at any time since we moved here fifty years ago."

The key element in this scenario is that new minister abandons the dream of waiting for the members to offer suggestions on a new direction and accepts the role as an active advocate of planned change initiated from within that organization. That role becomes acceptable by the combination of building trust by an intensive early effort in pastoral calling, listening, searching for allies, encouraging discontent with the status quo, creating an initiating group, and a patient emphasis on incremental change.

Expanding the Sunday Morning Schedule

Back in the first chapter we encountered the recently arrived senior pastor of a 119-year-old congregation who favored adding a second worship service to the Sunday morning schedule, but was facing resistance from that respected veteran leader, Otto Bohn, as well as others who favored the status quo.

One of that pastor's potential allies is the impatient Terry Winslow who advocates a combination of change-by-addition plus temporary systems. Terry's proposal calls for adding an early service without disturbing the rest of the Sunday morning schedule.

The new senior pastor has concluded the opposition is too strong to make that change without far more support than appeared to be present.

What is the issue here?

The pastor insists the central question is how decisions requiring change will be made in this tradition-bound congregation.

Otto Bohn contends the real issue is space. As long as that cavernous room is half empty on the typical Sunday morning, why even contemplate two services?

Terry Winslow urges, "Let's try it and see what happens."

Notably missing from this scenario are (1) substantial discontent with the status quo, (2) a statement of purpose by an initiating group that defines a goal that can be achieved only by revising the schedule, (3) a support group for that proposed change, and (4) a larger strategy that would include the new schedule.

Two means-to-an-end issues have been allowed to become the focal point for this discussion. One of these was raised by the new senior minister. How do we make decisions here? The second is the proposed new schedule. That discussion is further clouded by Otto's contention that the key variable is the ratio of attendance to the capacity of that big room.

A better approach could have been to create a long-range planning committee. That group might have discussed such issues as the low worship-attendance-to-membership ratio, the aging of the membership, the growing discontent with a highly traditional ministry of music, or the need to offer people a broader range of choices on Sunday morning as a means of reversing that long-time, gradual decline in attendance. Or they might have concluded that what once had been a high commitment parish gradually had drifted in the direction of low commitment. One component of a larger strategy to reverse that drift would be to project the expectation that every member would be present for both Sunday school and worship. A new schedule with worship at the first and third hours with a full-scale Sunday school in the middle period plus adult classes at all three hours would be consistent with a move toward high commitment.

In other words, the proposed new schedule should be seen as only a means-to-an-end issue hooked onto a larger policy question. That policy question, whether it be reversing numerical decline or reaching younger generations or a shift toward high commitment should be the focus of the discussion. The members of that discontented initiating group should define the issue in terms of purpose and ministry, not letting means-to-an-end issues dominate the debate.

In another congregation with an eighty-year tradition of Sunday school followed by worship, the recent growth produced an average worship attendance of 185 in a building that could comfortably accommodate two hundred at worship. To average 185 meant that on a dozen Sundays a year the room was packed with chairs in the aisles and behind the last row of pews.

When the suggestion to expand the schedule to two services first surfaced, it was greeted with loud disapproval. "That would split our church!" "We want to retain the feeling of one big family." "Being packed in is better than worshiping in a room that is half empty." "If we go to two services, it will be impossible for us to know everyone." "What would that do to our church?"

The ad hoc committee appointed to study the problem came back with this conclusion. "Given the recent growth of this congregation, the need for more space to accommodate more people for worship is clear. We have examined the three most attractive alternatives. One would be to sell this property, relocate to a new site, and construct a new building. We estimate the cost will be $2 million. The second would be to construct a new sanctuary on this site and remodel the old sanctuary into a second fellowship hall. We estimate that cost at $1.3 million. The third would be to expand the present schedule to provide for two worship services every Sunday morning. A fourth alternative, which we did not explore in detail, would be to send about forty of our younger families out to plant a new mission."

When this report was presented to a congregational meeting, the vote was 158 to 5 in favor of the revised schedule. The present schedule was not offered as an alternative. The people present chose from among four proposals for change and (naturally) picked the one that was least costly.

The Toughest Call of All

The Reverend Ross Hamilton came to the Hillcrest Church as the new minister of this 50-year-old, 243-member congregation in 1960. Eight years later, when he was killed in a tragic automobile accident, he left behind (1) a congregation of 591 members that had just moved into a big new addition to the original brick building, (2) a 38-year-old widow who was the part-time choir director, and (3) a large cadre of grateful leaders who felt a tremendous obligation to this minister and his widow.

One consequence was the unanimous decision of the congregation to name the new addition, "Hamilton Hall." A second was to offer the widowed Mrs. Hamilton a permanent part-time position as choir director.

A quarter of a century and seven ministers brought several changes. One was the recent marriage of Mrs. Hamilton to John Morris, the president of the local bank who had been widowed fourteen months earlier. Mrs. Hamilton and Mrs. Morris had become very close friends, and Mrs. Hamilton spent literally hundreds of hours with her dying friend during Mrs. Morris's terminal illness. This further endeared Mrs. Hamilton to many of the older members.

The next-to-the-last of this series of seven ministers had departed three years earlier when he told the pastoral relations committee, "I am interested in serving a church that has a future. This congregation faces a dim future as long as Mrs. Hamilton continues as the choir director. As many of you know, she undermined the ministry of my predecessor, and she has been busy undermining my ministry ever since the first day I arrived. Either she goes or I go."

After an hour's discussion of this unexpected ultimatum, the members thanked the minister for his candor and told him they had agreed by a 6-to-1 vote to accept his resignation.

His successor arrived just in time to officiate at the marriage of Mrs. Hamilton and Mr. Morris. Out of that shared experience the three quickly became close friends. Within a year or so, this new minister had concluded that he was confronted with a severe problem. Personally he and the new Mrs. Morris were good friends, but professionally they disagreed on almost every issue that arose.

During his second year the new minister talked with at least two dozen people about his problem. These included several former choir members, five of whom were now members of other churches in that community, with three of the previous organists, with the one person on the pastoral relations committee who had voted against accepting his predecessor's resignation, and with two respected and influential older women who had served in various leadership positions. One of the two now chairs the pastoral relations committee. He asked each of them several questions. One was, "Is it her or is it me?" They all assured him that (a) Mrs. Morris enjoyed great personal sympathy and popularity with the vast majority of the members and (b) he was far from the first to experience severe problems with her on the subject of church music.

One of the oldtimers declared she had been responsible for the departure of five of the six predecessors. "That's why people call the music department the war department," he explained.

Another explained, "If you want to survive here, you will have to get along with her, and that means you'll have to do 100 percent of the getting along."

By this time the membership had dropped by one-fourth and worship attendance was down by one-third from that peak back in 1968.

One day Martha Williams, the sixty-three-year-old respected leader who now chaired the pastoral relations committee came to see the pastor. "I just came from talking with our choir director. I suggested the time had come for her to step down and let someone else take over. She wouldn't hear of it. She hauled out the minutes of a board meeting from 1968 which reported she was to be named the permanent choir director, and she feels that means forever. What do we do next?"

"How do the other members of your committee feel about this?" asked the pastor.

"One is on her side, three, and that includes me, feel she must be replaced, and three lean toward replacing her, but they don't want a big battle over this," replied Mrs. Williams.

"Well, you folks picked her, I didn't," declared the pastor, "but it's now my problem as much as anyone's. I do not believe it is realistic to expect a standing committee like yours to resolve this. That is both unfair and unrealistic. Therefore I suggest you appoint a three person ad hoc committee that will be instructed to define the issue and prepare a recommended course of action. Ask that special committee to bring their report and recommendations to your committee and you will make a recommendation to the board."

Twenty minutes later the two had identified the three people who would be asked to constitute this ad hoc committee. One was a longtime friend of the choir director who also was one of the three members of the pastoral relations committee who believed the time had come for a change. One was a new member who had joined the choir eighteen months earlier and was perceived to be neutral. The third was a close friend of the pastor.

When Mrs. Williams brought the proposal to her committee, they were delighted to be able to pass the buck. All three nominees had agreed to serve and were appointed.

At their first meeting they spent a half hour with the pastor and Mrs. Morris, a half hour with the pastor, a half hour with Mrs. Morris, and a half hour reflecting on what they had heard.

A week later they met and spent two hours reflecting together and concluded the time had come for a change in choir directors.

Two weeks later they met with Mrs. Morris and explained to her, "We have agreed the time has come for a change. We appreciate your long and faithful service, but the time has come to write a new chapter with a new ministry of music and a new choir director. This evening we want to focus on three questions. First, the date of your retirement. Second, the terms of the termination. Third, the announcement of your departure. Do you prefer this be announced as your resignation or as your retirement?"

After several minutes, more than a few tears, but no harsh words, Mrs. Morris declared she wanted to retire, not resign.

Two days later Mrs. Williams received a telephone call filled with gratitude from Mr. Morris who thanked her and added, "For two years I've been trying to persuade her to retire, but she wouldn't listen to me. You may have saved our marriage."

A month later the best attended celebration in that congregation's history was held to honor, thank, and praise the retiring choir director.

Why Did It Work?

Why was that change made so smoothly?

1. The pastor refused to allow this to be perceived as a personal conflict between the new minister and the long-tenured and popular choir director.

2. The predecessor of the current minister had made at least a few people aware of the problem. Unfortunately for him, he stated the issue in terms of "win-lose" and thus made it easy for him to become the victim.

3. While his strategy was less than perfect, this predecessor's experience illustrates the point that sometimes change is possible only after it has been rejected at least once.

4. Nothing was done until after substantial discontent had surfaced.

5. The minister and the respected leader chairing the pastoral relations committee acted as an ad hoc initiating group of two to devise a response to the discontent.

6. The support group included respected and influential leaders—one of whom turned out to be Mr. Morris, but no one knew that in advance.

7. Sufficient time elapsed for some of the more reluctant members to talk themselves into the need for a change.

8. The responsibility to act was placed, not in a standing committee, but rather in a special ad hoc committee that had only the one assignment. Resolve the problem. The typical standing committee has many items on the current agenda so the members are tempted to focus on the easy ones and to postpone dealing with the difficult issues.

9. That ad hoc committee included one person who could understand the perspective of the choir director, the potential victim of change, as well as one member who could understand the perspective of the pastor, the potential victim of perpetuating the status quo. It also included one person who represented the choir, the group that would be most affected by a change.

10. That ad hoc committee stated the issue as "Resign or retire?" They did not state it as "Stay or resign?"

11. Everyone believes that any decision can be appealed at least once. By creating this ad hoc task force the pastoral relations committee became the first point of appeal, if an appeal was sought. That is far better than making either the board or a congregational meeting the place for an appeal on a personnel matter to be heard.

12. The big retirement celebration for the choir director was not only affirmation for her and her ministry, but it also was an act of reconciliation.

13. The pastor possessed the wisdom to be able to distinguish between professional incompatibility and personal compatibility. He kept the focus on the professional incompatibility. That reduced the temptation for people to choose sides in terms of personal popularity—a contest he would have lost, just as his

predecessor had lost when the issue was allowed to be viewed in that light.

14. The pastor was able to advise Mrs. Williams on how to make the system work, but also was able and willing to detach himself from that process and allow the three-member ad hoc committee to carry out their assignment.

15. Since this was a personnel matter, not a policy question, the members of the governing board trusted that committee to resolve the dispute. They did not barge in and grab for control. They allowed the system to work. One reason they chose to detach themselves obviously was cowardice. A second was they trusted the leadership of Mrs. Williams, and they trusted the competence and commitment of the members of that three-person ad hoc committee.

Trust is an essential component of an effective process for planned change!

Notes

Introduction

1. Those who want to read more widely on this subject would be well advised to turn to Richard Beckhard and Wendy Pritchard, *Changing the Essence* (San Francisco: Jossey-Bass Publishers, 1992). An exceptionally wise book on mandated change is Judith Hicks Stiehm, *Bring Me Men and Women* (Berkeley, Calif.: University of California Press, 1981). Two other outstanding books are Rosabeth Moss Kanter, *The Change Masters* (New York: Simon & Schuster, 1983) and Donald L. Kirkpatrick, ed., *How To Manage Change Effectively* (San Francisco: Jossey-Bass Publishers, 1985). The first, third, and fourth of these books were written largely to a business audience.

1. Covenant Community or Voluntary Association?

1. For suggestions on improving the teaching ministry, see Lyle E. Schaller, *44 Ways To Expand the Teaching Ministry of Your Church* (Nashville: Abingdon Press, 1992).

2. A more extensive discussion of cohesive forces can be found in Lyle E. Schaller, *Getting Things Done* (Nashville: Abingdon Press, 1986), chapter 3.

3. A delightful and provocative introduction to the concept of a third place is Ray Oldenburg, *The Great Good Place* (New York: Paragon House, 1989).

2. What Is the Climate?

1. One version of history claims that the reason G. Bromley Oxnam accepted election to the episcopacy in 1936 was that he was facing a faculty revolt at DePauw University. Robert Moats Miller, *Bishop G. Bromley Oxnam* (Nashville: Abingdon Press, 1990), pp. 189-191. Also see, "Sizing Up Colleges and Universities," *Change*, November/December 1990, pp. 35-38.

2. See Schaller, *44 Ways To Expand the Teaching Ministry of Your Church* (Nashville, Abingdon Press, 1992), pp. 38-41.

3. For comments on the role of the denomination as a regulatory agency, see the concluding essay by Craig Dykstra and James Hudnut-Beumler in Milton J. Coalter, et al., eds., *The Organizational Revolution: Presbyterians and American Denominationalism* (Louisville: Westminster/John Knox, 1992).

4. For suggestions on constructive responses to passivity, see Lyle E. Schaller, *Activating the Passive Church* (Nashville: Abingdon Press, 1981).

5. Schaller, *Getting Things Done*, chapter 7.

6. An even-handed account of this is Ronald J. Allen, "Kinnamon's Defeat and the Disciples of Christ," *The Christian Century*, December 11, 1991, pp. 1156-58.

7. This system of threefold visits is described in Lyle E. Schaller, *Hey, That's Our Church!* (Nashville: Abingdon Press, 1975), pp. 116-125.

8. Alvin Toffler, *Future Shock* (New York: Random House, 1970), pp. 324-29.

9. Schaller, *Getting Things Done*, chapter 6.

10. For a longer discussion of this trend, see Lyle E. Schaller, *The Seven-Day-A-Week Church* (Nashville: Abingdon Press, 1992), pp. 17-36.

3. Who Stirs Up the Discontent?

1. The selection and work of long-range planning committees is described in Lyle E. Schaller, *Create Your Own Future!* (Nashville: Abingdon Press, 1991).

4. Who Gave You the Authority?

1. Several of the implications of this are explored in Aaron Wildavsky, *The Rise of Radical Egalitarianism* (Washington, D.C.: The American University Press, 1991).

2. Robert A. Dahl, *After the Revolution? Authority in a Good Society* (New Haven, Conn.: Yale University Press, 1990), pp. 6-21.

3. Ibid., pp. 30-42.

5. Who Decides?

1. Dahl, *After the Revolution*, pp. 22-24.

2. Clark Kerr, *The Uses of the University* (Cambridge, Mass.: Harvard University Press, 1982), pp. 176-177.

3. Lyle E. Schaller, *44 Ways To Expand the Financial Base of Your Congregation* (Nashville: Abingdon Press, 1989), pp. 15-81.

6. What Is Your Strategy?

1. A heavy reliance on questions is one characteristic of an initiating leader. See Schaller, *Getting Things Done*, chapter 5.

2. Lyle E. Schaller, *44 Ways To Revitalize the Women's Organization* (Nashville: Abingdon Press, 1990), pp. 106-171.

3. Toffler, *Future Shock,* pp. 324-329.

4. Stiehm, *Bring Me Men and Women.*